Career,
aptitude and
selection tests

Career, aptitude and selection tests

Match your IQ, personality and abilities to your ideal career

3rd edition

Jim Barrett

London and Philadelphia

Whilst the author has made every effort to ensure that the content of this book is accurate, please note that occasional errors can occur in books of this kind. If you suspect that an error has been made in any of the tests included in this book, please inform the publishers at the address printed below so that it can be corrected at the next reprint.

Publisher's note
Every possible effort has been made to ensure that the information contained in this book is accurate at the time of going to press, and the publishers and author cannot accept responsibility for any errors or omissions, however caused. No responsibility for loss or damage occasioned to any person acting, or refraining from action, as a result of the material in this publication can be accepted by the editor, the publisher or the author.

First published in 1998 by Kogan Page Limited
Second edition 2006
Third edition 2009

120 Pentonville Road
London N1 9JN
United Kingdom
www.koganpage.com

525 South 4th Street, #241
Philadelphia PA 19147
USA

© Jim Barrett, 1998, 2006, 2009

ISBN 978 0 7494 5695 5

British Library Cataloguing-in-Publication Data

A CIP record for this book is available from the British Library.

Library of Congress Cataloging-in-Publication Data

Barrett, Jim.
  Career, aptitude and selection tests : match your IQ, personality and abilities to your ideal career / Jim Barrett. — 3rd ed.
    p. cm.
  ISBN 978-0-7494-5695-5
  1. Occupational aptitude tests. 2. Vocational interests—Testing. I. Title.
  HF5381.7.B673 2009
  153.9'4—dc22   2009016882

Typeset by Saxon Graphics Ltd, Derby
Printed and bound in India by Replika Press Pvt Ltd

Contents

Preface

To help readers benefit as much as possible from this book, I have provided explanations for the aptitude test questions. Where readers may have previously thought items were 'too difficult', I hope that, having understood those items better and having gained in confidence, they will feel enabled to perform at their best in future tests. I have altered some items where I have thought clarity in test items might be improved.

Introduction

This book has several aims:

1. To give career guidance

I believe that the more you know about yourself, the better your career choices are likely to be. In an increasingly competitive world, it seems sensible to know where you want to get to.

As far as this book is concerned, what is meant by 'knowing yourself' are those aspects which are relevant to work. It is thus a practical book, which presents a structured way to relate your various characteristics to career opportunities.

A word of warning here, right at the outset: although the book has a scientific basis, relating characteristics to career success is still something of an art. There are, of course, definite trends: in just the same way that people with certain likes or talents are better at one sport or game than another, so people's character-istics suit one occupation more than another. However, there are some people – and you may be one – who successfully go against the trend. Therefore, you should treat this book as a guide for your own thinking about your career. In no way does this book aim to provide a definitive solution as to what you can or cannot do.

I have provided some tests and questionnaires, relating these as best I can to different occupations. If you find that your results on the tests and questionnaires do not correspond with a career you believe would suit you, I trust you will not give up your own aspirations. For example, you may be suited to a career on the basis of combinations of characteristics that are different from but just as 'correct' as my own suggestions.

The combinations of motivational, aptitude and personality characteristics which can determine success in any job are enormous. Therefore, I have only listed those which have seemed sensible to me from my own experience. You will see the scheme presented in Section 4, Profile Matching. Use it to provoke your own thinking about your own characteristics, not as a check as to whether you have 'passed' or 'failed'.

The more you clarify your own ideas for yourself the better. Even though you may seek career guidance in this book, it can only be guidance. In the end, it is you who has to decide what makes sense to you, and it is you who has to take responsibility for the choices you make.

2. To prepare for selection situations

It is routine for organizations to give applicants for positions tests and questionnaires similar to those included in this book. They are also given to existing job holders in order to create awareness of potential development in the person's present job, or as a means of assessing suitability for other opportunities within the same organization.

By 'organizations', I mean many industries, businesses, public sector services and authorities, business schools, and so on. In short, it is almost impossible to get through your working life without some exposure to tests and questionnaires. The use of assessment processes based upon tests and questionnaires is expanding. Nowadays, they are administered by the majority of organizations. If you enjoy them, that is fine, but you are most unlikely to avoid them.

This being the case, there is every reason to become familiar with these various tools and processes. You should try to make them work for you as much as possible. The obvious way to start is to break down any fears you may have about the 'assessment' situation. The more familiar you become with these tools, the less likely you are to 'underperform' or to give an impression of yourself that is not the 'real you'. Putting yourself across in the way that allows assessors to perceive you clearly is as important in all assessment processes as it is at an interview.

Why do organizations use these tools? Quite simply, it is to reduce the risks attached to hiring or developing people who turn out to be unsuitable. The financial costs attached to wrong decisions on employment can be considerable. There are usually emotional costs to be taken account of as well. Anything that will increase the probability of success will be taken seriously by organizations.

3. To assist with performance at work

Broadly, there are two ways this book may assist you:

(a) To increase your personal effectiveness

Whatever career you are presently engaged in, or intend to join, you may want to use the opportunities that will exist in the organization to get the most satisfaction you can from your work. For example, your work may not always be just the way you want it. Perhaps the Motivation questionnaires will suggest that you should aim to get more of one type of activity in your work than another. Perhaps you have a personality which will suit doing the job one way rather than another. Perhaps you have a talent for which you do not have enough scope.

Changes in your career may often be achieved without changing the career itself. In many cases, it is seeking an adaptation to the present task, altering the balance of work responsibilities to create the preferred quality of work, rather than radically changing the entire career.

This book is based upon the premise that you are most effective when you are doing what you want and what you are capable of. Like everybody else, you are not fixed, and as you learn more about yourself and your potential, you will seek ways to fulfil yourself at work. The intention is therefore to provide a scheme which enables you to ask yourself whether there are things you want to do and can do that you are not yet achieving. Equally, the book might assist you to ask yourself what you would have to do to achieve what you want.

(b) To increase your effectiveness in working with others

Very few careers are purely technical these days. Although appropriate skills are as essential as they ever were, organizations place a great deal of emphasis upon how employees relate to each other. They know that good relationships at work can affect the speed at which tasks are accomplished as well as the quality of the task. These have a great impact upon the profitability of the organization and are therefore important to organizations, especially those that seek to remain ahead of their rivals.

Organizations which might assess you in this respect are generally far too sophisticated to want everybody to be sociable. Sometimes, they want people to be less sociable, because they have found that the job is done better this way. Salesmen might not need to be sociable, but may need to be socially assertive. Many highly effective leaders of companies that have thousands of employees are independent rather than sociable. What the organization wants is that you relate to others in a way which makes you an asset.

If you would like to read more about how to develop your personal and interpersonal skills in order to influence people, my book *Total Leadership*, is also available through Kogan Page.

Job suitability

One way of looking at personal effectiveness is to use this book to ensure that you get yourself into a situation that accords with your motivation, aptitudes and personality. Although people are sometimes reasonably satisfied simply to have a job, it is difficult to give it your best unless you are really doing what you want to do and can do best. In the short term, you may turn your hand to many activities, but in the long term it is frustrating if what you thought was a broad highway of career satisfaction turns out to be a cul-de-sac.

It is almost inevitable that you will seek to extend yourself as your career progresses. Don't wait until you become bored or frustrated. Don't blame others for not giving you opportunities. If this book enables you to pinpoint what it is that you want to achieve, then it is up to you to find a way to do what you want. If you are already in an organization, this adjustment is almost bound to be beneficial for the organization as much as yourself.

Teamwork

Due to the importance placed upon team working by organizations, this book presents you with a way of examining your personality and how your own 'style' may connect with others. There is no doubt that you have a style, and thus your behaviour has an effect upon others. Whether your behaviour always has the effect you wish, is for you to judge.

One way to understand your effectiveness is to see how your own style is different from those of other people. You may well become more effective as you learn to value people for their different styles, so that you see ways of complementing and compensating for each other.

You may also wish to change your style. This is perfectly possible. 'But', you may ask, 'does not this run counter to the view that personality is fixed and unchangeable?' Not at all. Though it is true that personality does not usually change over time – after all, people come to 'know us' and rely upon our continuing personal effectiveness – it is only awareness that is necessary to bring about change. Thus, if you see some aspects of your style as disadvantageous, you can certainly change these if you wish. Awareness of where you are now, and where you want to go, is the vital requirement.

In this book, Section 3 – Personality will show you a way to become more aware of your personal and interpersonal impact. Again, if you are keen to develop your awareness of your team effectiveness to a much greater degree, you should find my book *Total Leadership* provides you with the insights you need to do what you want.

Issues concerning testing

Here I would like to address some of the controversies which sometimes arise concerning testing, rather than in Section 2 – Aptitudes, where I would prefer you to be concentrating upon the tests. It is not at all necessary for you to read these comments before taking the tests, so miss this part out if you would prefer to get on.

The value of such a book as this is sometimes questioned, particularly with regard to the validity of aptitude testing. As with all sciences, there are contrasting theories and protagonists take up opposing positions, sometimes vociferously, often denying through their own behaviour the supposed rationality of science. The debates are occasionally reported in the press. Some theorists assert that there is no such thing as an aptitude, and that it is more proper to speak of learned responses. Others make the opposite assertion, that limits upon our achievements are determined by what we are born with.

The literature on learned versus inherited characteristics runs into tens of thousands of volumes. Recently, the evidence has been on the side of the genetic view which is that intelligence, and even specific types of intelligence, do not change over time. I do not intend to revisit all the research. In any case, from my point of view, it really does not matter.

I assume that people do have aptitudes which lead them to become better in one area of study or area of work than others. No other explanation suits my own experience of discovering people's potential. My job as a psychologist has only been to provide some suggestions as to how they might use it, if they want.

Many people are aware of their strengths and weaknesses. Sometimes people are not sure what they can do. Maybe they have had an education which has not exposed them equally to all those experiences that might have developed their awareness of what they can do. Maybe they have specifically been 'turned off' the pursuit of studies which suit their nature, perhaps by pedagogic limitations, parental expectations, geographic or circumstantial disadvantages.

I may have to remind you of what this book is trying to achieve. It is an invitation to people to think through their aptitudes and relate them to work opportunities. Everybody does this in any case. I am merely trying to provide a scheme – a 'tool', if you like – to assist their thinking. The scheme has limits; for example, there is not a test for musical potential. Those tests I have devised are representative of a universe of other possible tests.

The book does not intend in any way to be prescriptive. It suggests that, if you obtain a certain score on a particular test, you may have a leaning towards this or that career which is believed to have some relationship to the test. That is what is believed. It cannot be asserted with any finality, especially in the individual case, since there will always be some people who become successful in a career, contrary to any test result. This is the nature of statistics, where we are dealing with probabilities, not certainties. Thus, some mathematicians will be better with words than with numbers, even though we would assert that, as a general rule, more mathematicians will be better with numbers than words.

Therefore, care must be taken to allow for the point that, just because someone has not obtained a certain level on a test, or has a pattern contrary to that given in Section 4 – the Profile Matching section, it does not mean that they cannot succeed in that career. If they are determined and believe in themselves, and really do have the potential, though it may be different from what is presented in this section, they will be successful. Perhaps they will be more successful for having different aptitudes. Section 4 is only a guide; it serves as a basis for thinking through the issues; it may be altered over time if experience shows that other characteristics or scores are more suitable.

What happens if a person does not obtain an above average score on anything? It means that the process has not elicited an aptitude which is superior to other aptitudes within the person, or superior to the aptitudes of other people. This does not mean that the person does not possess aptitudes for different careers. Perhaps other tests might detect them. Perhaps the person might work hard in an area that motivates them, enabling them to perform at a level in 'real life' which is above that which is predicted by a short, timed test.

The tests are not, in the end, the 'real world' where 'success' depends upon so many factors that cannot be predicted by tests, such as a 'lucky break' or 'unique talent'. They are just tests. But that does not mean that they have no purpose either. In just the same way that we might at some point test the depth of the Pacific Ocean, we may gain some information which is more useful to us than simply accepting that it is useless to measure the depth of the Pacific because everybody knows that it is deep!

It would be arrogant to assert that the tests are absolute predictors of anything. They are tests, not final judgements about what people actually can or cannot do. They are intended to provoke thinking about possibilities in what is, after all, an eminently sensible, natural way – 'What are my strengths and weaknesses, how do they relate to a career?' and 'Do I have aptitudes which I am not taking account of?'

There is a view held by some experts involved with testing that it is unwise to allow people access to tests, since they might reach uninformed conclusions which might in some way be dangerous. I regard it to be a patronizing arrogance to withhold from people information about themselves, which they are perfectly capable of understanding and entitled to use as they wish. I suspect that many 'experts' are more intent upon protecting their own interests than the interests of the public.

Remember also that aptitude tests draw attention to the intellectual and practical potential of people who have failed in the education system. For example, the British Armed Forces routinely select and train educational 'failures' on the basis of aptitude testing, and continue to use this method because it is seen to work. So do many of our major industries.

It seems to me that a book that contains tests of aptitude fulfils a need many people have for information about themselves, which they often feel denied them during their education.

The mere experience of taking aptitude tests can be beneficial. This is because most people will be exposed to them at some time or other. The sooner they get used to them and understand something about them the better. This should help to dispel any fears and help them to do their best in what might be selection situations. On this side of the Atlantic, the use of aptitude tests to complement, or to replace, examination results, is increasing exponentially.

The process is, admittedly, far from perfect. This is why it must be clear that the guides given in Section 4 – Profile Matching, as well as in other sections, are only guides. In relation to the Profiles, I trust readers to work out for themselves how their own relative aptitudes relate to a career in a way that has as much credibility as my own suggestion.

Aptitudes and abilities

Aptitudes should not be confused with abilities. I admit these are often difficult to tease apart. Present-day capabilities are not aptitudes. Aptitudes are about 'potential', which is not necessarily realized at the present time.

To assert that aptitude testing is not useful at predicting anything seems to me to be a limiting, even dangerous opinion. If we adopt this view, we will never discover people with potential beyond the skills that have emerged thus far. Personally, I perceive the genetic view as the more positive one. There is much, much more in our genes than we are aware of. And, for me, the most valuable gene is the gene for imagination, because what we can imagine ourselves doing, we no doubt will.

Many people ask themselves if they have potential for things that they are not aware of at present. For the same reason as I would want to look at skills, which have emerged through experience, remembering that some people's experience is very different from that of others, so I would want to have an opportunity to look at potential in a similar way for everybody.

Aptitude testing is a way of attempting to put everybody on a level playing field. Even though there may never be such a thing, because life may never be like that, there are advantages in seeing what happens when we do. It is a way of attempting to 'take stock' of something which is usually affected, contaminated and distorted by so many other variables, in particular educational disadvantage or prejudice. It is a means of trying to ensure that there is some means to provide an opportunity for people to demonstrate the resources they have.

It is correct to say that, from day to day, people rely upon present-day knowledge and skills, but investigating whether there is potential that people are not aware of, is also correct. Often, the discovery of potential leads to the development of new interests. There is no need to rule one or the other out: they should be complementary.

Sometimes, there is a fear that test-takers may become discouraged, because they do not obtain the high scores they would like. If we treat tools as highly sensitive we may 'project' this sensitivity on to the test-taker. The more we can 'desensitize' the better.

The issue is often whether an average result on a test is lower than is expected. In the first place, the person may come to accept a realistic view of his or her potential. Thus, it may be better to succeed at a career which is just sufficiently demanding, than to continue to fail to obtain entry into a career which really is beyond their potential. Overambition can be stressful. However, there is nothing to stop them attempting, if that is their choice, to carry on and confound everybody's expectations.

In the second place, a low score may indeed mean that their potential has not been revealed by the tests. This will be due to the failure of the test to find that potential, either because the test does not detect their unique potential or because they did not impress themself upon the test on that occasion. They may do so at another time or seek evidence from other tests, or from alternative sources.

If a person thinks that aptitude tests do not detect his or her true potential, there always remain the conventional tests – examinations, interviews and work appraisal systems. Fortunately, in the end, whatever methods we might use to assist them, people do what they do. Some will find aptitude tests give them useful pointers, others will not.

Comparison

An individual's relative aptitudes make sense only in relation to others. To explain: you cannot say a person is better at words than numbers, unless that person is better at words than numbers when compared with others. Put another way, an individual is too few people upon which to obtain any meaningful information.

Inevitably, people and their aptitudes and abilities are compared with others. That is the way of the world.

This book intends to enable people to make an objective comparison of themselves with others on the basis of tests. The tests used here may not be the best tests for the individual person, but that is no reason why we should not use them, provided we are careful about the way we interpret them. Therefore, I trust I have given clear advice about the limitations as well as the advantages of testing.

However good the aptitude tests are, they are unlikely to be revealing unless certain conditions are met:

a) when they are given in the optimum conditions
b) when their results are expertly interpreted.

As far as a) is concerned, this will involve making sure that the test situation itself is properly controlled, including the administration and timing of the test.

A trained test administrator will do everything possible to ensure that the conditions in which you take the tests are the same as for everyone else with whom you might wish to compare yourself. It is a particularly difficult thing for you to do yourself since the situation in which you take the tests in this book is almost bound to be unique. As it may be impossible to remove the effect of many factors which might reduce your own performance, this is another good reason to view the results as giving you a guide, rather than telling you anything final about yourself.

As far as b) is concerned, proper interpretation is the province of an expert.

This book is an 'expert system' from which you are able to learn more about yourself, but it cannot present all the possibilities to you. To take one important consideration: it is only possible in this book to make an approximate comparison of your results with those of others. This is because the results you will be comparing yourself against are an estimate of what is likely to be an average score if everybody in the population were able to take the test. You would obtain more precise information about your potential, relative to others, if you were compared with a group of people who are representative of your age group, whose background and description could be closer to your own. It is not possible in this book to compare you with the exactly correct representative sample. Thus, one explanation for your obtaining a score of 'no evidence of this ability' might be that you are being compared unfairly.

On both points, a) and b), interpret the results with some latitude. In the final analysis, what you enjoy doing most – whatever the test results may say! – is probably the best guide. That said, I trust that a profile will emerge that has some meaningful, practical value for you.

With regard to Profile Matching at the end of the book, I make the point that the scheme that is presented contains suggestions. It is not intended to be prescriptive. The index is neither science nor law. The individual should consider how his or her own pattern of results might make him or her successful in the career that appeals – and, especially, in relation to the suggestions thrown up by the Motivation Questionnaires.

Companion volumes

Test Your Own Aptitude has been translated into several languages and is recommended by many Careers Services.

Other books of mine that have the same purpose and contain different types of test are *Aptitude, Personality and Motivation Tests, Advanced Aptitude Tests, The Aptitude Test Workbook* and *Numerical Aptitude Tests*.

Summary

This book was written for the test user to administer and interpret. Though the tests and questionnaires are 'proper' psychological tools, they are not written for restricted use by expert test administrators, though there is no reason why they should not also be used by experts. To the extent they may serve not only as a useful guide but also to demystify psychology, they will have achieved their purpose – allowing people access to information about themselves, which they are also perfectly capable of handling themselves.

1

Motivation

Introduction

It makes sense to match a person's interests to an occupation: it is difficult to succeed if you are bored.

Interests tend to develop because of our exposure to different sorts of experiences and also in relation to different talents which tend to find some outlet for their expression. Obvious questions arise from these circumstances: how do you know whether you would like a certain career when you have not yet had a chance to try it? How do you know that there is not some career which you have never thought about, but for which you may discover a talent when you try it?

In fact, through our education, reading, watching television, listening to the radio, and many other experiences, we have all had at least second-hand experience of many different forms of work. We are drawn to some more than others. True, we may not know ourselves as well as we could and may miss out on something which suits us. Or, maybe, there is more than one type of career that we are suited to. These are the sorts of reasons that lead many people to have more than one career.

The aim of this section is to assist you to see where your major interests lie at the present time. They may well change, although, in most people, interests, like personality and abilities, remain remarkably stable. Having established where your interests are, the objective is to relate them to different careers. The process is designed to assist you to choose from different avenues of opportunity. It is not only to get you started, or, for those who are thinking of a second career, into something which may appeal to you more than your present job, but to persuade you to consider the long-term benefits of choosing one area rather than another. To make a fully informed choice, you may also need to take your personality and aptitudes into account. These are subjects for later sections.

Getting the most from the motivation questionnaires

There are two questionnaires for you to complete. They use different ways to obtain relevant information about you. Neither questionnaire has 'correct' or 'incorrect' answers; there is no one way that is 'right' or 'best'. It depends what these words mean for you and what you want to gain from the questionnaire. Therefore, the way in which you 'see yourself' is important as you work through the questions. The most helpful results will probably emerge when you simply respond in the way that seems natural to you rather than as you think you 'should' or 'could' do. However, it is quite possible to take the questionnaires with different attitudes. The clearer you are in your own mind what these attitudes are, the more useful will be the results.

Career guidance

You could view the questionnaires as learning experiences in their own right. Thus, in the first questionnaire, you could look up and make sure you know what each of the various occupations actually involves before you respond to the item. That way, you will make a more informed choice. You will find books in the library to help you to do this. *Occupations,* published by CRAC, is a good one because it contains precise descriptions of different careers as well as other careers of a similar category. Another good reference is the *Dictionary of Occupational Titles*.

You could take a questionnaire simply on the basis of what appeals to you, not on the basis of whether you think you have the talent for it or not. This approach often works very well, because it establishes the nature of what you want to do. This approach makes the motivation questionnaires work like a personality test. Say the idea of being a musician appeals to you, but you know that all your attempts to learn a musical instrument have failed. What emerges from the questionnaire may well be a desire to pursue some expressive form or work, or to work in some way which allows you to be creative. So, although you might have said that you would like to be a musician, knowing that you could not be, the questionnaire may well reveal a career direction that is right for you. Motivation questionnaires, though they often appear rather simple and 'easy to fake' are actually rather complex instruments, if used properly.

You could equally well take a questionnaire on the basis of what you know you can, and cannot, do. Thus, you might leave out careers that demand a specialist degree or other qualification, if it does not look as though you would obtain them. Even so, the questionnaire might occasionally force you to choose between two activities, neither of which you might think could possibly be you. This 'forced choice' approach is intentional: in choosing a career, you will inevitably be forced to make choices which then preclude you from making other choices; in doing one thing, you will be unable to undertake another.

There is no reason at all why you should not ask others what they think you are capable of doing or what would suit you. You might find this to be revealing, especially when others' thoughts about your potential disagree with your own.

Job selection
Questionnaires like these are not only used for career guidance, but also for selection purposes by organizations to which you

might apply. They want to establish as quickly as possible whether your aspirations are going to be met by the job. There will be little point in your starting work if you and they discover that it does not really appeal to you. There is little point in you trying to fake such questionnaires in order to get the job either. You will not be helping yourself. Moreover, if your results look bizarre in comparison with your experience, you will have done yourself no favours. Far better to have established before your interview or other selection process that the occupation you are seeking is consistent with your own motivation.

Understanding your results

A word about the structure and composition of the questionnaire might be useful. As mentioned above, it takes a 'forced choice' format so that, in the end, you will have relatively strong interests in some areas and not in others. Occasionally, one or two people are interested in doing everything or in none of the activities within the questionnaire. Such results emerge, for different reasons, as 'middling', and will be dealt with later on under Interpretation. Most people have leanings to one area of work rather than another, and the structure of the questionnaire reveals this. The idea is that, although each career is different, each one falls roughly into a different, broad category. It is generally more useful to get the broad category right, since this keeps your options open, than identifying any single occupation.

The questionnaires are composed of different occupational titles and different descriptions of work activity. They are designed to establish what type of work might suit you. They are not selected on the basis of what level of work you might be capable of. You will be assisted further with this in Section 2 – Aptitudes.

The Motivation questionnaires are general questionnaires that encompass most types of occupations at all levels. If you are already a mature person and, perhaps, have already had a career with responsibility, maybe as a manager, you could be asked to complete a questionnaire designed specifically for managers when you go for an interview. Even though other questionnaires you take in specific circumstances appear to be more tailor-made for you, it is likely that the results will be very similar to those which emerge here.

Questionnaire 1. Job titles

You are asked to choose between different types of work. The aim is to see what sort of work appeals to you most.

Look at each group of jobs. There are seven in each set. Decide which one of the seven appeals to you most. Write the letter that goes with the job on the top line in the empty space next to number one. Then look at the remaining six jobs and see which one appeals to you most. Write this letter on the second line next to number 2. Then do the same with the other jobs. You will have sorted out the original list into your own, preferred list based upon which appeals to you most and least.

Obviously, as explained earlier, you could also do the questionnaire based upon what you think you 'can actually do' or 'would be capable of doing if you wanted', rather than simply upon what appeals to you.

Take no notice for the time being of the letters above the boxes on the next page. These are to assist you when you come to score the questionnaire. Their purpose will be explained later on.

Group A

			W	A	P	E	O	B	S
W	News reporter	1	___	...	...	...	...	...	...	...
A	Artist	2	___	...	...	...	...	...	...	...
P	Police driver	3	___	...	...	...	...	...	...	...
E	Food scientist	4	___	...	...	...	...	...	...	...
O	Local authority clerk	5	___	...	...	...	...	...	...	...
B	Business consultant	6	___	...	...	...	...	...	...	...
S	Occupational nurse	7	___	...	...	...	...	...	...	...

Group B

			W	A	P	E	O	B	S
S	Health care assistant	1	___	...	...	...	...	...	...
W	Freelance journalist	2	___	...	...	...	...	...	...
A	Clothes designer	3	___	...	...	...	...	...	...
P	Jockey	4	___	...	...	...	...	...	...
E	Nutritionist	5	___	...	...	...	...	...	...
O	Company secretary	6	___	...	...	...	...	...	...
B	Managing director	7	___	...	...	...	...	...	...

Group C

			W	A	P	E	O	B	S
B	Property speculator	1	___	...	...	...	...	...	...
S	Junior teacher	2	___	...	...	...	...	...	...
W	Publishing coordinator	3	___	...	...	...	...	...	...
A	Print designer	4	___	...	...	...	...	...	...
P	Train driver	5	___	...	...	...	...	...	...
E	Engineer	6	___	...	...	...	...	...	...
O	Accountant	7	___	...	...	...	...	...	...

Group D

			W	A	P	E	O	B	S
O	Building society clerk	1	___	...	...	...	...	...	...
B	Political agent	2	___	...	...	...	...	...	...
S	Osteopath	3	___	...	...	...	...	...	...
W	Stage or film critic	4	___	...	...	...	...	...	...
A	Pop musician	5	___	...	...	...	...	...	...
P	Hotel porter	6	___	...	...	...	...	...	...
E	Hydrographic surveyor	7	___	...	...	...	...	...	...

Group E

			W	A	P	E	O	B	S
E	Electronics designer	1	___	...	...	...	...	...	...
O	Medical records clerk	2	___	...	...	...	...	...	...
B	Fund raiser	3	___	...	...	...	...	...	...
S	Infant teacher	4	___	...	...	...	...	...	...
W	Drama teacher	5	___	...	...	...	...	...	...
A	Three dimensional designer	6	___	...	...	...	...	...	...
P	Steward/stewardess	7	___	...	...	...	...	...	...

Group F

			W	A	P	E	O	B	S
P	Refuse operative	1	__	...	...	...	...	...	....
E	Laboratory technician	2	__	...	...	...	...	...	...
O	Distribution manager	3	__	...	...	...	...	...	...
B	Glazing salesperson	4	__	...	...	...	...	...	...
S	Educational psychologist	5	__	...	...	...	...	...	...
W	Historian	6	__	...	...	...	...	...	...
A	Model maker	7	__	...	...	...	...	...	...

Group G

			W	A	P	E	O	B	S
A	Art historian	1	__	...	...	...	...	...	...
P	Construction worker	2	__	...	...	...	...	...	...
E	Astrophysicist	3	__	...	...	...	...	...	...
O	Building society officer	4	__	...	...	...	...	...	...
B	Personnel director	5	__	...	...	...	...	...	...
S	Remedial teacher	6	__	...	...	...	...	...	...
W	Librarian	7	__	...	...	...	...	...	...

Group H

			W	A	P	E	O	B	S
W	Scriptwriter	1	___	...	...	...	...	...	...
A	Film editor	2	___	...	...	...	...	...	...
P	Shoe repairer	3	___	...	...	...	...	...	...
E	Microbiologist	4	___	...	...	...	...	...	...
O	Marketing statistician	5	___	...	...	...	...	...	...
B	Advertising account executive	6	___	...	...	...	...	...	...
S	Psychotherapist	7	___	...	...	...	...	...	...

Group I

			W	A	P	E	O	B	S
S	Field social worker	1	___	...	...	...	...	...	...
W	Legal officer	2	___	...	...	...	...	...	...
A	Art gallery assistant	3	___	...	...	...	...	...	...
P	Heavy goods vehicle driver	4	___	...	...	...	...	...	...
O	Travel agent	5	___	...	...	...	...	...	...
E	Statistician	6	___	...	...	...	...	...	...
B	Stallholder	7	___	...	...	...	...	...	...

Group J

			W	A	P	E	O	B	S
B	Area sales manager	1	__	...	...	...	...	...	...
S	Probation officer	2	__	...	...	...	...	...	...
W	Speech therapist	3	__	...	...	...	...	...	...
A	Classical musician	4	__	...	...	...	...	...	...
P	Police constable	5	__	...	...	...	...	...	...
O	Finance clerk	6	__	...	...	...	...	...	...
E	Software programmer	7	__	...	...	...	...	...	...

Group K

			W	A	P	E	O	B	S
E	Surgeon	1	__	...	...	...	...	...	...
B	Record producer	2	__	...	...	...	...	...	...
S	Play leader	3	__	...	...	...	...	...	...
W	Barrister's clerk	4	__	...	...	...	...	...	...
A	Soloist	5	__	...	...	...	...	...	...
P	Lifeguard	6	__	...	...	...	...	...	...
O	Computer operator in commerce	7	__	...	...	...	...	...	...

Group L

		W	A	P	E	O	B	S
O Accounting technician	1 __	...	...	...	...	...	...	...
E Dental surgery assistant	2 __	...	...	...	...	...	...	...
B Sales assistant	3 __	...	...	...	...	...	...	...
S Community education worker	4 __	...	...	...	...	...	...	...
W Interpreter	5 __	...	...	...	...	...	...	...
A Session musician	6 __	...	...	...	...	...	...	...
P Gardener	7 __	...	...	...	...	...	...	...

Scoring the questionnaire

Look at your responses to Group L above and then to all the other groups. Where you have written in a letter against each number, place the number under the corresponding letter. For example, if this was your response to Group L:

Example – placing of letters

		W	A	P	E	O	B	S
O Accounting technician	1 _P_	...	...	...	...	...	...	...
E Dental surgery assistant	2 _S_	...	...	...	...	...	...	...
B Sales assistant	3 _W_	...	...	...	...	...	...	...
S Community education worker	4 _A_	...	...	...	...	...	...	...
W Interpreter	5 _O_	...	...	...	...	...	...	...
A Session musician	6 _E_	...	...	...	...	...	...	...
P Gardener	7 _B_	...	...	...	...	...	...	...

Then, to complete your scoring for the group, it would look like this:

Example – placing scores in columns

			W	A	P	E	O	B	S
O	Accounting technician	1 _P_	...	...	1...	...	...	...	...
E	Dental surgery assistant	2 _S_	...	...	...	...	...	...	2...
B	Sales assistant	3 _W_	3...	...	...	...	...	...	...
S	Community education worker	4 _A_	...	4...	...	...	...	...	...
W	Interpreter	5 _O_	...	...	...	...	5...	...	...
A	Session musician	6 _E_	...	...	...	6...	...	...	...
P	Gardener	7 _B_	...	...	...	...	...	7...	...

This needs to be completed for each of the groups, A to L. Then you can add up all the points you have collected in each of the seven columns under each of the seven letters. It may look like this:

Example – totals of columns

W	A	P	E	O	B	S
20	16	74	70	62	32	52

You need to mark your own scores in each group and then add the scores in all the columns. Place your scores in the box below:

Your scores for Motivation questionnaire 1

W	A	P	E	O	B	S
...	...	...	...	...	...	...

Place your scores, with a mark or small circle, at the appropriate point in the chart below.

Motivation chart 1. Job titles

	low	average	high
Type	84–80–75–70–75–65	60–55–50–45–40	35–30–25–20–15–12
W – words	– – – – –	– – ' – –ı –	– – – – –
A – artistic	– – – – –	● – – – –	– –∤ – –
P – physical	– – – – –	∤ – – – –	– – – – –
E – experimenting	– – – – –	– – –ı – –	– – – – –
O – organizing	– – – – –	∔ – – – – '	– – – – –
B – business	– – – – –	– – – –ı –	– – – – –
S – social	– – – – –	– –ı – – –	– – – – –

To finish off, join up your small marks or circles so that there is a line running between them. Now you have a chart showing your areas of preferred and least preferred types of career.

Questionnaire 2. Job activities

The next part asks you to choose between two activities. Look at each pair of jobs or job descriptions. You have 3 points to share between the two in the way that will show how much they appeal to you. If one appeals to you a great deal, you would give all 3 points to that one, and no points to the other. If one appeals to you slightly more than the other, give 2 points to that and 1 point to the activity you prefer less. The points you decide to award must be written in the boxes opposite the job descriptions.

Take no notice for the time being of the letters above the box. These are to assist you when you come to score the questionnaire. Their purpose will be explained later on.

Example 1

a Farmer	a <u>0</u>
or	
b Clerk	b <u>3</u>

In Example 1, being a clerk obviously appeals, while being a farmer does not appeal at all.

Example 2

a Songwriter	a <u>2</u>
or	
b Salesperson	b <u>1</u>

In Example 2, it has been more difficult to make a choice. However, the points have been divided to show that, on balance, being a salesperson does not appeal so much as being a songwriter. Remember, you must allocate 3 points, either 3 and 0, or 2 and 1.

As explained earlier in relation to the first questionnaire, you could do the questionnaire based upon what you think you 'can actually do' or 'would be capable of doing if you wanted', rather than simply upon what appeals to you.

Take no notice for the time being of the letters W, A, P, E, O, B, S in the answer space. These are to assist you when you come to score the questionnaire. Their purpose will be explained later on.

		W	A	P	E	O	B	S
1 a	Use machines to shape objects and bore holes or			a_				
1 b	Gather information about insurance claims					b_		
2 a	Decide upon the lighting effects for filming or		a_					
2 b	Undertake routine servicing of vehicles			b_				
3 a	Recover information about ancient civilizations or				a_			
3 b	Recommend savings or other financial products					b_		
4 a	Edit letters for inclusion in a magazine or	a_						
4 b	Sell second-hand goods for a profit						b_	
5 a	Install electrical wiring in buildings or			a_				
5 b	Investigate insurance claims for possible fraud					b_		
6 a	Undertake developmental checks on the health of children or							a_
6 b	Lay cables for the installation of telecommunications equipment			b_				
7 a	Provide for the holistic care of a patient or							a_
7 b	Play in a band			b_				
8 a	Support people with learning difficulties and their families or							a_
8 b	Have responsibility for the operation of an oil rig			b_				
9 a	Make individual dresses for special occasions or			a_				
9 b	Select the best stories for inclusion in a book	b_						

	W	A	P	E	O	B	S
10 a Direct a drama or	a_						
10 b Diagnose and repair faults in domestic cookers, microwaves or fridges			b_				
11 a Obtain information about investment for use by brokers and fund managers or					a_		
11 b Train people to sell various goods						b_	
12 a Guide people and answer questions in a museum or		a_					
12 b Rivet or bolt pieces of metal together			b_				
13 a Maintain cash limits on hospital purchasing or					a_		
13 b Teach dance classes		b_					
14 a Experiment on the way memory functions or				a_			
14 b Design the interior of an important new building		b_					
15 a Make appointments for, and retrieve files for, patients or					a_		
15 b Give advice, support and comfort to upset people							b_
16 a Rehabilitate employees who have been ill or							a_
16 b Work in the field of genetic engineering				b_			
17 a Pay pensions or other allowances to the public or					a_		
17 b Produce images for a stage production		b_					
18 a Persuade people to vote for or support your political or charity campaign or						a_	
18 b Write speeches	b_						
19 a Write science fiction or	a_						
19 b Administer the business of a company					b_		
20 a Design a set for a theatre or		a_					
20 b Translate ancient languages	b_						
21 a Ensure production targets are met by planning and controlling resources or			a_				
21 b Sell insurance over the telephone or by personal visit						b_	

	W	A	P	E	O	B	S
22 a Build confidence in injured people by helping them to learn new tasks or							a_
22 b Fit together components to make finished products			b_				
23 a Clear and sell the contents of houses or						a_	
23 b Undertake research applying mathematical modelling				b_			
24 a Process meat or fish in a factory or			a_				
24 b Write about professional theatre productions	b_						
25 a Find ways to advertise your company's products or						a_	
25 b Help children who have a learning difficulty							b_
26 a Examine the nutritional aspects of food or				a_			
26 b Manipulate limbs to relieve pain or tension							b_
27 a Specialize in costume design or		a_					
27 b Run a newspaper						b_	
28 a Extract and purify metals from ore or				a_			
28 b Write scripts for TV programmes	b_						
29 a Study fossils or				a_			
29 b Run a newspaper and sweets shop						b_	
30 a Write instructional pamphlets or	a_						
30 b Map and analyse an area of ground to look at soil and vegetation characteristics				b_			
31 a Write articles on your own subject for publication or	a_						
31 b Set up a mutual support group for people who have similar difficulties							b_
32 a Speak on behalf of others about political matters or						a_	
32 b Stitch or glue leather together			b_				

	W	A	P	E	O	B	S
33 a Look after elderly people in a residential centre or							a_
33 b Be in charge of a payroll department					b_		
34 a Act in a TV commercial or	a_						
34 b Seek to understand the causes of a criminal's behaviour in order to redirect it positively							b_
35 a Set up and run a pay policy or					a_		
35 b Write a brochure for a place which is a tourist attraction	b_						
36 a Use dyes in the production of textiles or carpets or			a_				
36 b Analyse ocean movements to better understand world climate				b_			
37 a Sell water purification systems or						a_	
37 b Take photographs of people		b_					
38 a Make travel arrangements and assist in the planning of conferences or					a_		
38 b Investigate causes of fires and reconstruct accidents				b_			
39 a Write a book for art lovers or		a_					
39 b Give tests or questionnaires to assess a pupil's career aims and abilities							b_
40 a Prepare trial balances or audit accounts or					a_		
40 b Be the owner of a cleaning or catering company						b_	
41 a Work on the interior design of a hotel or		a_					
41 b Design lasers for use in surgery and for other scientific use				b_			
42 a Encourage students to take an active part in their learning or							a_
42 b Direct the financial resources of a business						b_	

Scoring

Add column totals.

	W	A	P	E	O	B	S
Column totals							

You need to add the scores in all the columns. Place your scores in the box below under the appropriate letter:

Your scores for Motivation Questionnaire 2

	W	A	P	E	O	B	S
	...	...	...	...	...	...	...

Place your scores, with a mark or small circle at the appropriate point in the graph below. Join up the points with a line so that you can see clearly what your preferences are.

Motivation chart 2. Job activities

	low			average			high		
Type	2 4 6	8 10		14 16 18	20 22		24 26 28	32 34	
W – words	–	–	–	–	–	–	–	! –	–
A – artistic	–	–	–	–	–	– !	–	–	–
P – physical	–	– !	–	–	–	–	–	–	–
E – experimenting	–	–	–	–	–	!	–	–	–
O – organizing	–	–	–	–	! –	–	–	–	–
B – business	–	–	–	–	! –	–	–	–	–
S – social	–	–	–	!	–	–	–	–	–

Comparing results on motivation

Most people do not obtain striking differences on the two questionnaires, but if you have some, how much significance should be placed upon them? Large differences would indicate that the activities appeal to you more than the job titles, or job titles more than the activities. So, for example, it would be as though you are rejecting the idea of certain jobs, but like the sound of the nature of the work itself. This may be due to a lack of understanding of what the jobs actually involve.

In this case it would be worth doing some investigation as to what is involved in certain occupations you may be unclear about, especially if it is an area where the second questionnaire indicates there could be an interest.

Now you can choose one or both of the questionnaire results to see the types of career to which your results might lead.

Interpretation

The seven areas of work motivation form a scheme derived from three more fundamental areas: the arts, the sciences and the humanities. Also, the seven areas flow into each other, so that they are connected in a logical way. This is the scheme:

	Primary interests	Combined interests	Mixed interests
Arts	social words art	social and words words and art art and physical	social and art social and physical social and experimenting words and physical art and experimenting
Sciences	physical experimenting	physical and experimenting experimenting and organizing	physical and organizing physical and business experimenting and business experimenting and words

continued overleaf

	Primary interests	Combined interests	Mixed interests
Humanities	organizing business social	organizing and business business and social	organizing and social organizing and words organizing and art business and words business and art

You can see, in the second column of the chart, that social is in the arts as well as the humanities. This is because the primary areas of interest also form a circle, so that each area flows into the next. Thus, words are used as an art, art may also be visual or musical before it becomes a craft and more physical. Then, the material, physical area becomes more analytical or experimenting in science. In turn, the scientific area becomes numerical and flows into finance and other areas of organization. This leads into business, then into the social areas and, eventually returns once again through communication to words.

If you have a single high score, then you have a primary interest. This does not mean that what you do will not include other areas; far from it. All it does is to show where your major interest will be. All other interests are likely to be used to support it. You will need to look at what your next highest scores are so that you can have some chance of using them as well in your work. Also, look at your lowest scores, because these are the least important to you, so you are unlikely to enjoy a career so much if it places undue emphasis upon these.

If you have two high scores, you will either have a combined score or a mixed score. It is usually possible to find a career which combines interests. Mixed scores are, of course, also combined, but they are from different, sometimes opposite ends of the spectrum, so that the activities of this mixed type are often quite varied and are sometimes difficult to bring together. Sometimes there can be a conflict as to what the main interest in a mixed career is, for example, an art teacher may at times find a delicate balance between love for the subject and dedication to pupils.

It is quite possible that you have three or more high scores which contrast with your low scores. There are many permutations of three, four, five or six high scores. In such cases, you will have to ask yourself what your high scores represent and how you can join all your interests in a single career. It is usually possible. For example, if your interests are experimenting, organizing and social, this might mean that you want work that is mathematical, in the business world, where you are involved with people. Accountancy or actuarial work could be suitable. Some other possibilities will be found in the Profiling Section at the end of this book.

If all your scores are in the average range you may have much in common with highly talented people who often seek a career which has numerous aspects. Often, managing directors of businesses get a flat pattern of interests. It does not mean they have no interests, but rather than they want a very broad job which involves them in some way with everything that is going on. If you are already a managing director, that is fine, but this is not much help if you are looking for career direction. In this case, it is probably a good idea to take the questionnaire again and this time be very strict with yourself about what is realistically possible for you. In such a situation, it may be wise to consult a career counsellor. It is worth mentioning that if you have not yet started work, it is a good idea to consult a careers counsellor in any case.

Primary areas of motivation

The examples given below are those which often correspond with the interest area. Remember that many other factors always need to be taken into account. For example, architects may have a strong interest in the art area, but may also need to be interested in involving themselves in business and organization. Thus, some of the examples will appear in more than one area.

W – Words

You will use words in your career whatever you do. In fact, you will already be an expert in the use of words simply from your experience of everyday living. However, if this is your high preference, it means that you want to make the business of words the means of making your living, not as an adjunct to some other activity.

You may have enjoyed English or other 'wordy' subjects, such as history, at school. Your aim may be to use words creatively or you may be drawn towards careers which in some way involve you with information and communication.

Few people have the talent to make a living on the basis of their creative writing. More structured and predictable careers arise in journalism or public relations. There are other careers which are often suited to this area of preference, such as legal work and librarianship.

Examples

actor/actress	journalist
creative writer	language teacher
editor	librarian
historian	literary critic
interpreter	proof reader

A – Art

A preference in this area almost invariably indicates that you want to use your imagination and express yourself through art, music or dance. At a deeper level, it can often suggest, even though a person may not be artistically gifted, that he or she wants a career which allows freedom and the opportunity to use intuition.

Whatever form of art you pursue, it is likely to contain plenty of hard work and dedication. The discipline required by artists is frequently unappreciated by those outside artistic professions. Also, many careers in art are relatively low paid, which is surprising in view of the length of time needed to study for qualifications.

There are some people who are fortunate to become popular with comparatively little effort. So much in this area depends upon 'what the public wants' and whether you happen to be 'at the right place at the right time'.

Most creative careers do not carry any guarantees of security and income. Work may depend upon the piece of work you produce or may be linked to a short contract. More security of tenure exists if you work on a permanent basis as a member of a design team in a shop, with a manufacturer or in some other organization. These opportunities also give you more continuing contact with others. This is an important point, since many artists are prepared to follow a style of life which requires a great deal of self-reliance.

Examples

architect	interior designer
artist	make-up artist
dancer	musician
dressmaker	sculptor
engraver	silversmith
florist	vision mixer
goldsmith	window dresser
illustrator	

P – Physical

This area covers work where you might be physically active, perhaps engaged in sport or working outdoors. At one end of the spectrum, physical work might be delicate, even artistic, while at the other it might be heavy, involving large equipment or machinery. It might require skills which are visual as well as mechanical.

If you score highly in this area it is likely that you want to achieve something which is concrete. You might want to work by yourself on a task involving materials. Alternatively, you may want to use your experience and common sense in understanding and interacting with the environment. In this case, you may want to work alone and are prepared to do so often under harsh, sometimes dangerous conditions.

Examples

animal handler	guard
baker	gunsmith
boat builder	instrument maker
builder	jockey
butcher	joiner
carpenter	locksmith
coastguard	mechanic
cook	merchant seaman
diver	miner
driver	nature conservancy warden
farmer	oil rig worker
fisherman	park ranger
fitter	plumber
forester	shipping pilot
gamekeeper	traffic warden
groom	upholsterer
groundsman	veterinary nurse

E – Experimenting

What probably appeals to you about this area is the opportunity to acquire knowledge and to analyse results. These interests suit you to science since you enjoy observing, recording and making deductions.

Careers in this area require habits of study and precise work. An ability with mathematics is the common link with most although, if your interest is biology, you may be less mathematically grounded than if your interest is physics. Work in all the sciences is changing as rapidly as technology changes, so that new opportunities for experimentation arise through increasingly powerful computers. Although science appears to be dependent upon instrumentation, it still requires the same enthusiastic curiosity.

Many areas of science are desperately short of qualified people while in others it is difficult to get a job even with a higher degree.

Examples

astronomer	materials scientist
bacteriologist	mathematician
botanist	meteorologist
chemist	microbiologist
dietician	opthalmist
ergonomist	physicist
experimental psychologist	radiographer
forensic scientist	surgeon
laboratory technician	

O – Organization

This area is about administration. It could include financial matters, as well as legal ones. It is relevant to all institutions whether in the public or private sector since it involves the effective use of resources – whether people or materials.

Since this area is concerned with making sure that decisions are carried out properly, you will need to coordinate the efforts of others. Your own approach will need to be structured and orderly. People who organize, whether it is in a small office or a large enterprise, often have enormous influence, simply because they are the ones who know most about what is going on. As a consequence, such positions also carry a good deal of responsibility. This is why qualifications are increasingly sought in aspirants for senior positions. However, it is still possible to learn through experience and there is no doubt that if you have the right potential you will get on. In larger organizations, senior positions are most likely to be occupied by people who have professional qualifications in banking, insurance, accountancy or similar.

Examples

accountant	clerk
accounting technician	company secretary
actuary	fund society manager/assistant
administrator	legal executive
auditor	purser
bank clerk	records clerk
bursar	securities analyst
cashier	tax inspector

B – Business

If this is your highest preference you will be motivated by the chance to earn your living your own way. It is not about working by yourself, but working for yourself. This is true even if your business is running somebody else's business on their behalf. Without a doubt, people who are most successful in this area run the business as if it were their own, whether it is or not. The responsibility and rewards for this type of career include all the attendant risks associated with failing to live up to the expectations people have of you and the specified or assumed promises you have made to them. For sure, in this career you are expected to have personal qualities of drive and determination.

The especially attractive feature of this area is that it is open to anybody, regardless of qualifications, though leaders of large businesses almost always seek to acquire qualifications in order to improve their performance further. Whatever the size of business you work in, being able to spot an opportunity, together with the will to succeed, are still the essential attributes.

Examples

broker	negotiator
business consultant	personnel director
business person	political agent
exporter/importer	politician
management consultant	retail manager
managing director	sales manager
marketing manager	

S – Social

Though every career involves contact with others at some point, your objective is to make people your focus. A high score in this area reveals how much you are prepared to assist others in their development. Your career may range from giving advice to devotedly caring for people who are unable to help themselves.

Such careers are seldom easy and sometimes require an extreme measure of personal resourcefulness. For example, social workers who have the best of intentions sometimes have to make decisions on behalf of others which cause stress to everybody concerned, whether professional or client. Before entering a career in this area it is as well to gain experience to make sure it is right for you.

Success in this area depends upon personal judgement. Tact, patience and understanding are commodities you must have in abundance. A 'tough skin' is often required in situations where you may receive few thanks for your efforts. Of course, the rewards of seeing people improve make these careers worthwhile.

Examples

ambulance crew	midwife
careers adviser	nurse
childcare officer	nursery nurse
chiropodist	osteopath
educational psychologist	physiotherapist
health visitor	probation officer
hostel warden	remedial teacher

industrial nurse	social worker
medical practitioner	teacher

Combined interests

Social and words

You will be interested in careers that combine ideas, people and communications. Obvious possibilities are in teaching though other areas might involve you in some form of business, for example, public relations.

If you are more concerned with the literary side, then language skills may be more important to you than the caring, social side. On the other hand, a speech therapist may have skills in linguistics, though the primary aim is to help others overcome difficulties rather than acquire knowledge.

Examples

interviewer	speech therapist
language teacher	training officer

Words and art

You appear to seek knowledge and the chance to express ideas, often in novel ways. It is unlikely that you will be satisfied by a more conventional career. Therefore, the way you work and what you do will often be envied by others who will admire the variety and lifestyle you appear to have. Such careers are not without risk so perhaps the most important asset to have is a belief in yourself and what you are doing.

Examples

actor/actress	film reviewer
advertising copywriter	TV production assistant
dramatist	voice-over artist
film director	

Art and physical

This area gives you the chance to apply art in a practical way. An example would be the potter, whose sense of proportion and design is wedded to a useful object. There are many crafts which combine beauty with practicality.

There are also attendant opportunities if you look beyond the task itself. For example, your talent might lead to a business, or it could take you into the social area, through teaching or therapy.

Examples

bookbinder	embroiderer
cabinet maker	flyman (theatre)
cake maker	gardener
camera person	pattern cutter
confectioner	pattern maker
curtain maker	picture framer
dresser	potter
embalmer	

Physical and experimenting

This area will involve you with the application of science. You are the person who takes the theory and makes it work in practice. Such careers demand knowledge and experience. Often, people rely upon you more than they know, and what you do is essential to a secure and comfortable existence.

Examples

agriculturist	hydrologist
biomedical engineer	instrument maker
computer engineer	metallurgist
engineer – production, mechanical, civil, aeronautical	navigating officer

environmental health officer   surveyor
ergonomist   technologist
geologist   work study officer
horologist

Experimenting and organizing

You may be interested in mathematics, statistics, finance or marketing, and other areas which combine your interest in figures with an analytical approach. If your interest is statistics, you are more likely to be on the scientific side. If your interest veers more to actuarial, then you will probably prefer to work in a business organization.

Careers which combine the two areas very well indeed, and where there are expanding opportunities, are in systems areas. It is possible to be involved with systems integration as well as systems development within an organization. In these cases, you would be expected to have skills on the social side as well.

Examples
business systems analyst   market researcher
chief actuary   operations researcher
computer programmer   statistician
economist   systems analyst

Organizing and business

You are likely to be astute and commercially minded. You will enjoy the thought of working within organizations such as banking, insurance, finance and administration. You will need to be a good manager, first of all in managing the efforts of others and also in managing systems and resources. Whereas many business-minded people are quite intuitive, you are more controlled and factual. Your knowledge about how business works, together with your drive for efficiency, are likely to mean you are a force to be reckoned with.

Examples

bank manager	office manager
club manager	tax consultant
estate manager	turf accountant
insurance manager	underwriter

Business and social

You will want to work with and for people, but not in a personal, caring way. Instead, your efforts are likely to be more detached, though, sometimes, on a grander scale. Thus, you might achieve a great deal for others through your business sense. You may show your concern by creating the circumstances or the resources through which others are enabled to care in a more direct way. You are more likely to head the committee which obtains the resources that patients need than be a skilled helper yourself. Your obvious talents are more likely to be political than sensitive, though there is no doubt that the latter are present as well.

Examples

charity manager	job interviewer
funeral director	retail manager
head teacher	salesperson
hospital manager	social services director
hotel manager	

Mixed interests

Social and art

Careers that combine these areas require skills in relation to both the subject and to people. A great deal of sympathy, warmth and patience are required in order to communicate with others and help them. Many careers in this area are undertaken by volunteers, who often have extensive experience and insight to bring to their work. This is unlikely to be the correct area for you if your aim is to do great things with your art. Instead, you would want to use your subject in the service of others, a very selfless activity.

Examples

art therapist

music therapist

nursery teacher

occupational therapist

Social and physical

You would want to be active, working with others in order to achieve a definite task. Your tendency is to 'go for it'. The way you approach your work will depend on whether you are something of an organizer or whether you are more artistic. In the former case, you may be drawn to areas of industrial production. In the latter case, you may enjoy sports coaching or aerobics teaching. If your other, supporting interests are more towards business, then you may like to be in charge of some team work or operation management. Your enthusiasm and ability to work with others usually mean you will be an effective leader.

Examples

hairdresser

masseur/masseuse

occupational therapist

police officer

prison officer

production supervisor

sports coach/assistant

team coach

youth leader

Social and experimenting

If these are your interests, you will probably want to apply expert knowledge in the service of others. You may well be consulted for advice, but your relationship with others is more likely to be professional and detached than emotionally involved. Your background will be in science, but your intention will be to direct that science to others' welfare or education.

Examples

clinical psychologist

dental assistant

dentist

nurse

orthoptist

radiographer

science teacher

social science researcher

Words and physical

These two areas are generally mutually exclusive: although most of us are active and communicating with each other most of the time, there are few careers which combine them specifically. The writer of technical books or the sports writer are examples which show how the two can come together, but these are very highly specialized careers. How can you get started? It will be worth looking at the words and physical areas separately, at the same time thinking whether any careers in these areas will give you enough scope for your other interest. Also, consult the Profile Matching section (at the end of the book) where some other alternatives may be found.

Examples

printer	sports writer
secretary in agriculture	technical writer

Art and experimenting

You will want scope in your career to combine your interests in an expressive medium as well as analysis. Clearly, you have a desire to use science and technology to create something of perfection. You may well come up with some innovative ideas yourself. It seems that whatever work you do, some creative or technical challenge is important.

Examples

archaeologist	fine art restorer
beautician	lighting technician
car stylist	medical illustrator
cartographer	museum assistant
designer	photographer

Physical and organizing

If these are your interests, then you will want a career which requires you to implement and get things done. You probably like to work in a moving environment. You may like to be 'out and about' yourself. Ensuring that resources, goods or equipment are getting to the right place at the right time is something which you will be interested in. Increasingly, careers in this area will involve you in costing and budgeting in order that deadlines can be met.

Examples

baths manager	manufacturing team leader
builder's merchant	organization and methods officer
customs officer	rating valuation officer
IT technician	works manager
logistics manager/ transport manager	

Physical and business

You want to combine an interest in business with the chance to be out and about, or to become actively involved with what is happening. You may like to be on a site or involved with property. You might enjoy buying and selling equipment or stock. Typically, you will be practically minded, making things happen or turning your hand to most things.

Examples

accident assessor	farm manager
auctioneer	production manager
demonstrator	publican
domestic engineering manager	undertaker
estate agent	

Experimenting and business

These preferences seek to combine the intellectual with the material. It is sometimes possible, as is shown by the number of chemists (pharmacists) who venture into retail. Of course, science is big business, so many of the largest companies, such as drug companies, have huge teams of scientific researchers. Those who make it to the top of these organizations start out in science, but have developed a strong streak of business enterprise along the way.

Examples

director of scientific research company	retail pharmacist
dispensing optician	technical representative
IT consultant	veterinary surgeon
medical representative	

Experimenting and words

Your interests lie in the realm of ideas, communication and intellectual challenge. You will like to acquire knowledge for which you may perceive novel applications. You may lack the practicality to turn ideas into reality, but you may inspire others to do so.

Examples

anthropologist	science writer
archaeologist	technical writer
information scientist	

Organizing and social

You want to work with others as part of an efficient team. People may well look to you for leadership, since you appear willing to do the necessary paperwork and scheduling. Although your administrative and personal skills may be useful in most organizations, particularly in business, you seem likely to derive most satisfaction when your work has an altruistic element. You work well in a community or public institution where you experience a sense of purpose from assisting others.

Examples

courier/local representative   medical secretary
employment officer   principal nursing officer

Organizing and words

It may be that you enjoyed literary subjects at school, but decided that you were more commercially minded than academic. Broadly, your preferences will direct you towards careers which are administrative. You will no doubt be involved with communications and probably the management of others as well. These careers may not have much in the way of a literary or creative content, but may have great variety and scope for expression in a practical way.

Examples

administrator (clerical/executive) library assistant
barrister   receptionist
company secretary   secretary
entertainment officer   solicitor
legal executive

Organizing and art

You are seeking a creative environment as well as responsibility for getting things done. You might enjoy working in a fast-paced, hectic job where the end result nevertheless has to be a superb performance.

Examples

box office clerk   props manager
chef   receptionist
choreographer   studio assistant
cinema manager   theatre administrator
front of house manager   wardrobe manager
merchandiser

Business and words

Your own background might be literary and you might enjoy writing. However, your greater interest is to combine your liking for books and ideas in business. Also, you might be drawn to a career where you are 'in the spotlight'. In this case, your career might be connected with communications.

Examples

conference executive	public relations executive
literary agent	publisher
newspaper editor/manager	radio, TV or film producer

Business and art

These preferences almost always signify a desire to have a varied, enterprising career. You will enjoy a career which involves you with design or with the media. You like ideas and will seek opportunities for some original expression. You will probably be quick to spot something, either material or an idea, that will appeal to others. Often, you can arrange these things in a way that demonstrates the appeal of what you have discovered.

Examples

advertising account executive	fashion buyer
art dealer	media director
brand manager	salesperson

Aptitudes

Introduction

This is the largest section of the book, containing seven different tests. The reason for including so many are that they are each separately connected to a way of reasoning, and thus to an area of work. At the same time, whether you are stronger on one test than another leads to the possibility that you may perform better in one area of work than another.

Due to the fact that the tests are comparatively simple, and areas of work much more complex, it is quite possible that the tests will reveal your potential imperfectly. If you think about it, most careers demand many different aptitudes. Again, the same career for different employers may require aptitudes to be expressed in different ways. So, even if the tests do reveal your 'true' potential, there remains the difficulty of how to 'match' these to a career.

Yet, because everything we accomplish in the world is the product, ultimately, of our internal, mental process, it is sensible to use what methods we can in an attempt to establish what we can do. This will help to ensure that we are not overlooking some aspect of our potential that could be developed.

It would be possible to include many other tests. Examples would be tests of musical potential, dexterity, colour coordination, for instance. On these tests, you may gain results which are different from, or add to the picture given by, those you take here. Those that have been included owe their presence to the assumption that they cover the majority of careers.

Tests of aptitude can be controversial. But the tests are not included for this reason, but because they are intended to be enlightening. They are also included in order to give you practice in understanding a process that most people will go through many times during their time at school and at work. These issues have been dealt with in the Introduction, if you are interested in such debate.

Some people like to take tests because of the enjoyment they obtain from simply doing them. It does not matter to them what their score is, since it is the challenge that they are after.

Some people like taking tests in order to improve their Intelligence Quotient (IQ). The truth is that it is their ability to do better on tests that they improve. But this makes a very important point: if your score on any of the tests is lower than you think it should be, that is, you think you have performed 'badly', remember that this score most reliably reflects your lowest potential. You should not be saying, 'That score is bad,' but, 'I am at least that good.' You might do better on another occasion, or on different tests.

At the same time, the point of the exercise is to ask yourself what your results mean. For example, lack of success on one of the tests may well point to an area of weakness, while stronger scores on another test may point to areas of study or work which will be comparatively easy for you. Most people enjoy using their strengths rather than their weaknesses. In the end, if you think you are stronger in areas where the tests suggest no particular strength, you should pursue your own idea.

Remember that the aim is to make you think about what you do relatively well and less well. If your own thinking leads to an evaluation which is different from what is suggested from your taking these tests, or from the Profile Matching section at the end of the book, that is all to the good. In the end, it is your own interpretation of yourself that counts the most.

The tests are presented in no particular order; do them in any order you like. It is not necessary to do all of them, but most benefit is obtained if you do, since you then gain a 'profile' which shows your relative potential. The individual tests and the profile will have most meaning if you follow the instructions carefully.

General instructions

When taking the tests, ensure that you have a place you can work quietly without interruption.

You will need an accurate watch. One that 'counts down' is preferred. Also make sure that the light is good and that you have pencils and rough paper to work on.

Read the instructions carefully and read them as many times as is necessary, not starting the test before you are clear about what you have to do. This is most important, as you will waste time if you have to turn back to read the instructions once you have already started.

You have to do as many items as you can in the time allowed. Do not try to rush through to get everything done in the time allowed. If you do so, you are likely to make mistakes, because the tests have been designed to be almost impossible to finish within the short time given.

Work as quickly and as carefully as you can. Try not to guess. On these tests, guessing will not count against you, provided you get the correct answer. On other tests you might take, random guessing counts against you, so it unwise to guess at items if you can possibly avoid it.

How to interpret your scores

After you have completed the test, you can check your answers to see how many were correct. Then you can see how well you did by referring to the chart. Your score will fall into one of four grades, comparing you with other males and females who also took the tests. The grades are:

ne – no evidence of aptitude (IQ up to 100)
se – some evidence of aptitude (IQ range 101–114)
ge – good evidence of aptitude (IQ range 115–124)
ee – exceptional evidence of aptitude (IQ range 125+)

Some interpretation is possible on the basis of each test. Further interpretation is possible as more test results are obtained.

As a guide to what the grades mean in practice, 'ee' would indicate that a person might have the potential to perform at degree level where this aptitude was relevant. If you have 'ge' then you may be slightly less academically minded. A grade of 'se' suggests the presence of an aptitude to use in a career. You will see how this system works later on when you come to the section dealing with Profile Matching.

How 'high' is my 'IQ'?

The tests in this book are not only wide ranging – having been designed to examine different types of aptitude – but also measure a wide 'IQ' range, which extends well into the range showing excellent evidence of potential. Although it may not seem necessary to see if your aptitude may be truly exceptional (if for example your result shows an 'IQ' of 135) there is significant interest here for many people. If you want to get an idea of just how high you can go, you can get an estimate of your individual and combined 'IQ' on pages 145 and 146.

Verification

In this test you have to pay careful attention to a string of information. The string follows a regular pattern, but has been broken somewhere in the middle. You have to discover what is missing where the string is broken.

Look at each string of letters, numbers or symbols. You will see that there is a pattern that is repeated. What characters are missing from each of the following examples? Choose from the alternatives provided.

Examples

a.

A A B B C A A B B C A B B C A A B B C A A B

a) A   b) B   c) C   d) A A   e) B B   f) C C

b.

4 5 3 3 4 5 3 3 4 5 3 4 5 3 3 4 5 3 3 4 5

a) 3   b) 4   c) 5   d) 3 4   e) 4 5   f) 3 3

c.

□ ○ ⌇ □ □ ○ ⌇ □ □ ○ ⌇ □ □ ○ ⌇
□ □ ○ ⌇ □ □ ○ ⌇ ○ ⌇ □ □ ○ ⌇ □

a) ⌇   b) ○   c) □   d) □□   e) ○○   f) ⌇□

In example a) the repeated sequence is two As, two Bs and a single C. You can see that there is a point in the middle of the line where the sequence is not completed correctly. The letter A has to be added to follow the rule of repeated sequence in the line. Therefore, the letter A must be chosen from the list of alternative answers. You should underline or circle the answer 'a)'.

In example b) the repeated sequence is two 3s, a 4 and a 5. This is true even though the sequence does not start at the beginning of the line. A 3 is missing from the sequence in the middle of the line. Therefore, you should have underlined or circled answer 'a)'.

In example c) the sequences continue into a second line. The sequence is two squares, a circle and two wiggly lines. Two squares are missing from a sequence in the second line. Therefore, you should have answered 'd)'.

You have to work quickly in the time given, but it is important not to make mistakes. You have 10 minutes. Begin when you are ready.

1.

A B A B A B A B A B B A B A B A B

a) A A   b) B   c) C   d) A   e) B B   f) B A

2.

2 1 2 1 2 1 2 1 2 2 1 2 1 2 1 2

a) 1 2   b) 2 2   c) 2 1   d) 4   e) 2   f) 1

3.

■ O O ■ O O ■ ■ O O ■ O O ■ O O

a) ■   b) O   c) □   d) ■ ■   e) O O   f) O ■

4.

A B C A B C A B C A B A B C A B C

a) A   b) B   c) C   d) A A   e) B B   f) C C

5.

1 5 1 5 1 5 1 5 1 5 1 5 5 1 5 1 5

a) 1 5   b) 4   c) 5 1   d) 1 5 1   e) 5   f) 1

6.

□ ○ ♒ □ ○ ♒ ○ ♒ □ ○ ♒ □ ○ ♒

a) ♒   b) ○   c) □ ♒   d) □ □   e) ○ ○   f) □

7.

B C C A B C C A B C A B C C A B C C A B C

a) C   b) B   c) A B   d) A   e) B B   f) A C

8.

7 6 8 7 7 6 8 7 7 6 8 7 7 6 8 7 7 6 8

a) 6 8   b) 6   c) 7 7   d) 7   e) 5   f) 8

9.

♒ ♒ □ ○ ♒ ♒ □ ○ ♒ ♒ ○ ♒ ♒ □ ○

a) ♒   b) ○ ○   c) □   d) □ ♒   e) ○   f) ♒ □

10.

T J T J J T T J T J J T T J T J T T J T J J T

a) T   b) T J   c) J T   d) J   e) T T   f) J J

11.

6 1 6 3 3 6 1 6 3 3 6 1 6 3 3 6 1 6 3 3 1 6 3 3 6

a) 3 3   b) 6   c) 1   d) 3   e) 1 6   f) 6 1

12.

♎ ♒ ♋ ♋ ♎ ♎ ♒ ♋ ♋ ♎ ♎ ♒ ♋ ♋ ♎ ♒ ♋ ♋
♎ ♎ ♒ ♋ ♋ ♎

a) ♎   b) ♎ ♎   c) ♒   d) ♋   e) ♎ ♋   f) ♒ ♋

13.

R C E D E R R C E D E R R C E D E C E D E R

a) R   b) C E   c) D   d) R C   e) E   f) R R

14.

3 6 1 6 3 3 6 1 6 3 3 6 1 6 3 3 6 1 6 3 3 1 6 3 3 6

a) 3 3   b) 6   c) 1   d) 3   e) 1 6   f) 6 1

15.

□ ♌ ♎ □ □ ○ □ ♌ ♎ □ □ □ ○ □ ♌ ♎ □ □
♌ ♎ □ □ □ ○ □ ♌ ♎ □ □ □ ○ □ ♌ ♎ □ □ □ ○ □
♌ ♎ □

a) □   b) ○ □   c) □ ♌   d) ♌   e) ♎   f) ○

16.

C C A B B C C B C C A B B C C A B B C C A B

a) A   b) B A   c) C   d) A B   e) B B   f) C C

17.

3 3 8 1 3 8 1 1 3 3 8 1 1 3 3 8 1 1 3 3 8 1 1 3 3 8

a) 1 3   b) 3 3   c) 1   d) 8   e) 1 8   f) 3 8

18.

□ ● □ ● ● □ □ ● □ ● □ ● □ □ ● □ ● ● □ □ ● □
● ● □ □ ● □ ● ● □ □ ● ● □

a) ●   b) ● ●   c) □ ●   d) □ □   e) ● □   f) □

19.

W R Y W Y R S W R Y W Y R S W R Y W Y R S W
R W Y

a) W   b) R   c) Y   d) S   e) S R   f) R Y

20.

2 2 8 2 3 2 8 2 2 8 2 3 2 2 8 2 3 2 8 2 2 8 2 3 2 8
2 2 8 2 3 2 8

a) 8   b) 2 3   c) 3 3   d) 2 8   e) 8 2   f) 2

21.

● ♒ ● □ □ ● ♒ ● □ □ ● ● ♒ ● □ □ ● ● ♒ ●
□ □ ● ● ♒ ● □ □

a) ● ♒   b) ● ●   c) ● □   d) □   e) ●   f) □ ●

22.

R T Y U R T Y U R T Y U R T Y U R T R T Y

a) R   b) Y T   c) U   d) Y U   e) Y   f) R R

23.

6 9 6 3 7 3 6 9 6 3 7 3 6 3 7 3 6 9 6 3 7 3 6 9 6 3
7 3 6 9

a) 6 9   b) 7 3   c) 9 6   d) 3 7   e) 9   f) 6

24.

♎ ⊠ □ □ ♋ ♋ ♎ ⊠ □ □ ♋ ♋ ♎ ⊠ □ □
♋ ♋ ♎ ⊠ □ □ ♋ ♋ ♎ ⊠ □ ♋ ♎ ⊠ □ □

a) ♋ ♎   b) ♋   c) □   d) □ ♋   e) ⊠   f) ⊠ □

25.

B T B Y S B T B Y S B T B Y S B T B Y S B T Y S B T

a) B Y   b) S   c) B T   d) T   e) B   f) Y

26.

4 7 7 4 6 7 6 6 4 7 6 7 6 6 4 7 7 4 6 7 6 6 4 7 7 4
6 7 6 6 4 7

a) 7 4   b) 7 7   c) 6 6   d) 4 7   e) 9   f) 6 7

27.

□ ♋ ♋ ♎ □ □ ♋ ♎ ♎ □ ♋ ♋ ♎ □ □ ♋ ♎
♎ □ ♋ ♋ ♎ □ □ □ ♋ ♎ ♎ □ ♋ ♋ ♎ □ □ □ ♋
♎ ♎ □ ♋ ♋ ♎ □ ♋ ♎ ♎ □ ♋ ♋ ♎

a) ♎   b) ♋ ♎ ♎   c) □ ♋   d) ♋   e) □   f) ♋ □

28.

T B E S B T E S B T T B E S B T E S B T T B E S B
T E S B T T B E S B T E S B T T B E S B T E S B T
T B E S B S B T T B E S B T E S B

a) T E   b) S B   c) B T   d) E S   e) T   f) T T

29.

7 9 1 2 7 4 1 7 9 1 2 7 4 1 7 9 1 2 7 4 1 7 9 1 2 7
4 1 7 9 1 2 7 4 1 7 9 1 2 7 4 1 7 9 1 2 7 4 9 1 2 7
4 1 7 9 1 2 7 4 1 7 9 1 2 7 4 1 7 9 1 2 7 4 1 7

a) 1 7   b) 7 4   c) 1 2   d) 2 7   e) 9 1   f) 4 1

30.

□ ♋ ♎ □ ♒ ♎ □ ♋ ♎ □ ♒ ♋ ♎ ♎ □ ♋ ♎ □
♒ ♋ ♎ ♎ □ ♋ ♎ □ ♒ ♋ ♎ ♎ □ ♋ ♎ □ ♒ ♋
♎ ♎ □ ♋ ♎ □ ♒ ♋ ♎ ♎ □ ♋

a) ♎ ♒   b) ♋ ♎   c) □ ♒   d) ♒ □   e) □ ♋   f) ♎ □

31.

S S G I S G I G R B S I R G S S G I S G I G R B S
I R G S S G I S G I G R B S I R G S S G I S G I G R
B S I R G S S G I S G I G R B S I R G S S G I S G I
G R B S R G S S G I S G I G R B S I R G S S G I S
G I G R B S I R G S S G I S G I G R B S I R G S S
G I S G I G R

a) G I   b) I R   c) S   d) G   e) R   f) I

32.

1 0 7 1 3 7 1 0 7 1 3 8 3 7 1 0 7 1 3 8 3 7 1 0 7 1
3 8 3 7 1 0 7 1 3 8 3 7 1 0 7 1 3 8 3 7 1 0 7 1 3 8
3 7 1 0 7 1 3 8 3 7 1 0 7 1 3 8 3 7 1 0 7 1 3 8 3 7
1 0 7 1 3 8 3 7 1 0 7 1 3 8 3 7 1 0

a) 3   b) 8 3   c) 1 0   d) 0 7   e) 3 8   f) 7 1

33.

♎ ◆ ♍ ◆ ♏ ♍ ◆ ♏ ♑ ♍ ❖ ❖ ♎ ◆ ♍ ◆ ♏
♍ ◆ ♏ ♑ ♍ ❖ ❖ ♎ ◆ ♍ ◆ ♏ ♍ ◆ ♏ ♑
♍ ❖ ❖ ♎ ◆ ♍ ◆ ◆ ♏ ♑ ♍ ❖ ❖ ♎ ◆
♍ ◆ ♏ ♍ ◆ ♏ ♑ ♍ ❖ ❖ ♎ ◆ ♍ ◆ ♏

a) ♏ ♍   b) ◆ ♏   c) ❖ ♎   d) ♍ ❖   e) ♍ ◆   f) ♑ ♍

34.

P L O K K O L P L P L K P L O K K O L P L P P
O L K P L O K K O L P L P P O L K P L O K K O
L P L P P O L K P L O K K O L P L P P O L K P L
O K K O L P L P P O L K P L O K K O L P L

a) P O   b) P P   c) K O   d) O   e) P   f) L O

35.

3 2 9 5 9 5 6 3 6 6 5 9 2 6 3 2 9 5 9 5 6 5 9 2 6 3
2 9 5 9 5 6 3 6 6 5 9 2 6 3 2 9 5 9 5 6 3 6 6 5 9 2
6 3 2 9 5 9 5 6 3 6 6 5 9 2 6 3 2 9 5 9 5 6 3 6 6 5
9 2 6 3 2 9 5 9 5 6 3 6 6 5 9 2 6 3 2 9 5 9 5

a) 6 6   b) 3 6 6   c) 6 3 2   d) 9 5   e) 6 6 5   f) 6 3 6

36.

❖ ♌ ❖ ♍ ○ ○ ■ ○ ❖ ♍ ⊠ ⊠ ♍ ❖ ❖ ♌ ❖ ♍ ○
○ ■ ○ ❖ ♍ ⊠ ⊠ ♍ ❖ ❖ ○ ○ ■ ○ ❖ ♍ ⊠ ⊠ ♍
❖ ❖ ♌ ❖ ♍ ○ ○ ■ ○ ❖ ♍ ⊠ ⊠ ♍ ❖ ❖ ♌ ❖ ♍
○ ○ ■ ○ ❖ ♍ ⊠ ⊠ ♍ ❖ ❖ ♌ ❖ ♍ ○ ○ ■ ○ ❖
♍ ⊠

a) ⊠ ♍   b) ♍ ❖ ❖   c) ♌ ❖ ♍   d) ♍ ⊠   e) ❖ ♍ ○
f) ❖ ♌ ❖

Marking the test of verification

1. d)	2. f)	3. e)	4. c)	5. f)	6. f)
7. a)	8. d)	9. e)	10. d)	11. b)	12. a)
13. f)	14. b)	15. b)	16. d)	17. a)	18. c)
19. c)	20. e)	21. e)	22. d)	23. c)	24. d)
25. e)	26. a)	27. e)	28. a)	29. a)	30. b)
31. f)	32. b)	33. a)	34. a)	35. b)	36. c)

Number correct = _____ + (3 if there were no mistakes)

= _____ Total score

Score

no evidence	some evidence	good evidence	excellent evidence
IQ range up to 100	IQ range 101–114	IQ range 115–124	IQ range 125+
1–7	8–15	16–23	24+

Interpretation

This type of test is used to find out whether the test taker is likely to make errors in a task that appears deceptively simple, repetitive and, possibly, even boring. But it is also a demanding intellectual task because of the attentive focus required as well as the capacity to work with increasingly extended strings of information. Examples would be in administrative and IT-related tasks. It is the type of aptitude that is demanded to perform many types of work where attention to detail is essential, especially where any mistakes may be difficult to trace at a later date; for example, if mistakes creep in to original programming they may well become 'bugs' later on.

Formation

This test explores how easily you can see how shapes fit together.

You are to answer each question with 'Y' for 'Yes' and 'N' for 'No'. Write 'Y' or 'N' next to the number of the answer. If you prefer, mark with a tick or cross.

You will be shown a shape in the middle of the page. This shape is made up of two or more sections. Below the shape are five smaller figures. You have to decide which of these five figures will fit *exactly* into one of the sections in the shape.

It is important to remember that, to be correct, the figure must fit *exactly* into the shape. The figure will be correct even though it may have been turned around, upside down or turned over. It must have the same height, thickness and size and *exactly* the same angles. Try to 'see' the completed shape in your mind.

Example:

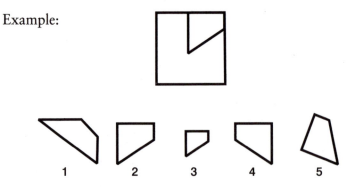

Answer 1 is wrong because it will not fit *exactly* into the small or large space in the main shape. Answer 2 is correct because it fits exactly into the small space in the main shape. Answer 3 is too small. Answer 4 will fit exactly, even though it has been turned over. Answer 5 has been turned around, but will also fit exactly into the small space.

Your answers to example items should be:

1 N   2 Y   3 N   4 Y   5Y

You have to work as quickly and as accurately as you can. You have 8 minutes. Start as soon as you are ready.

1.

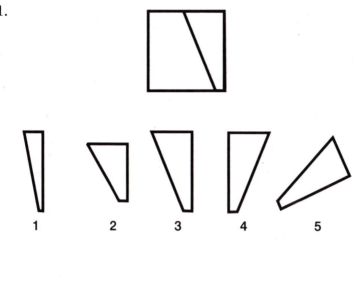

2.

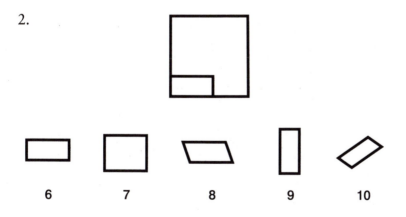

3.

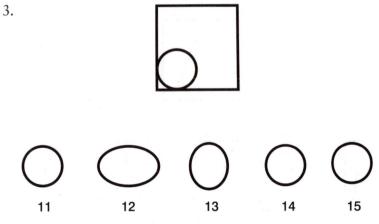

11   12   13   14   15

4.

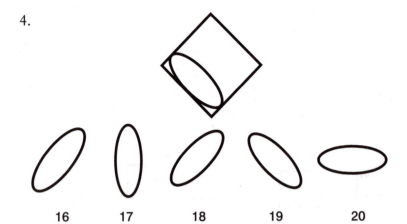

16   17   18   19   20

5.

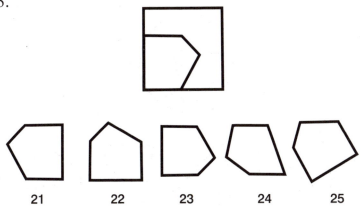

21   22   23   24   25

6.

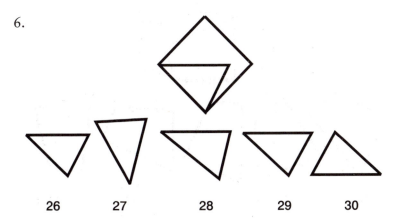

26   27   28   29   30

7.

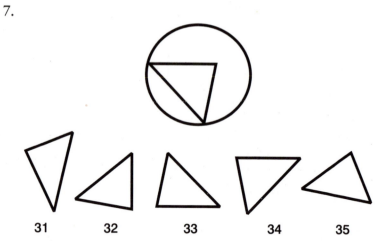

8.

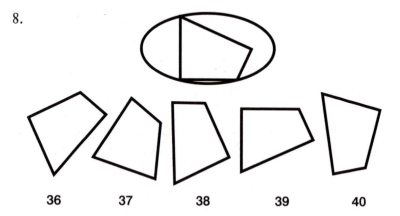

9.

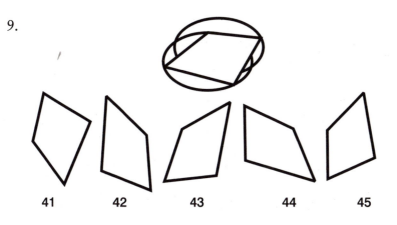

41   42   43   44   45

10.

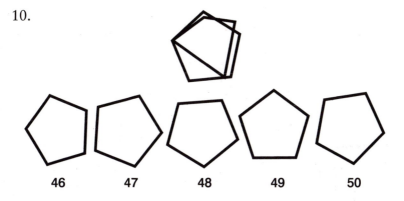

46   47   48   49   50

11.

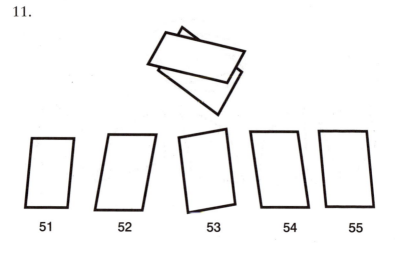

51 52 53 54 55

12.

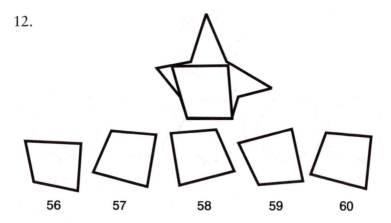

56 57 58 59 60

13.

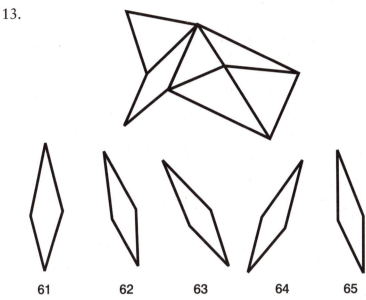

14.

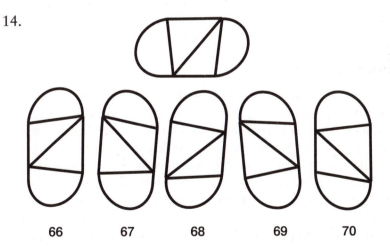

Marking the test of formation

1 – N	2 – N	3 – Y	4 – Y	5 – Y	6 – Y
7 – N	8 – N	9 – Y	10 – N	11 – Y	12 – N
13 – N	14 – Y	15 – Y	16 – N	17 – Y	18 – Y
19 – Y	20 – Y	21 – Y	22 – Y	23 – N	24 – N
25 – Y	26 – N	27 – Y	28 – N	29 – N	30 – Y
31 – N	32 – N	33 – N	34 – N	35 – N	36 – Y
37 – N	38 – Y	39 – Y	40 – Y	41 – Y	42 – N
43 – Y	44 – Y	45 – N	46 – N	47 – Y	48 – N
49 – Y	50 – Y	51 – N	52 – N	53 – N	54 – N
55 – Y	56 – N	57 – Y	58 – Y	59 – N	60 – N
61 – N	62 – N	63 – Y	64 – Y	65 – Y	66 – Y
67 – N	68 – Y	69 – Y	70 – N		

Number correct = _____ + (4 no mistakes) – (half mistakes)
= _____ Total score

Score

no evidence	some evidence	good evidence	excellent evidence
IQ range up to 100	IQ range 101–114	IQ range 115–124	IQ range 125+
1–10	31–38	39–46	47+

Interpretation

This test requires you to hold an object in your mind, while also turning it upside down, around and pulling it out of shape. The ability to do this is associated with success in the area of design, where a sense of shape and form would obviously be required.

The test of formation can also have wider implications. For example, it requires a flexibility of thinking to be able to recognize an object in a form which may or may not be the same as the original.

To be able to perceive the various components of a problem in new ways is an intellectual process which is useful in electronic engineering and other 'high-tech' computer and electronic sciences. Aptitude on this test, therefore, may indicate an 'artistic' design potential, but may also indicate an engineering or technological aptitude.

Physical analysis

This tests your understanding of forces and dynamics. It shows your understanding of mechanical and other physical principles.

There is a written question and a diagram. Together, they contain all the information you require to answer the question.

Choose the correct answer from the alternatives you are given. You can place a 'tick' by the correct answer or, if you prefer, put a circle around it.

Example

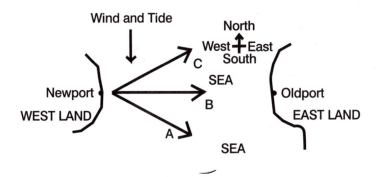

A sailing boat leaves Newport, which is about 10 kilometres west across the sea from Oldport. Both the wind and tide are towards the south. Which direction should the boat be headed in order to have the shortest journey?

a) A   b) B   c) C

The answer is 'C'. Going in direction A or B would mean that the boat would be pushed by the wind and tide towards the south, so the boat would have to turn and head north in order to arrive in Oldport. Heading in direction C counters the effect of the wind and tide, keeping the boat on the shortest route between the two ports.

Now go on to the test. You must work as quickly and as accurately as you can. You have 15 minutes. Begin as soon as you are ready.

1.

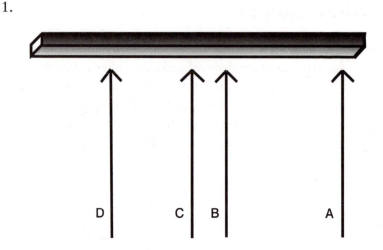

A beam is supported at the points shown by the four supporting arrows, A, B, C and D. Which two arrows could be removed so that the beam remains in the same position?

a) D and C   b) A and C   c) A and B   d) any two

2.

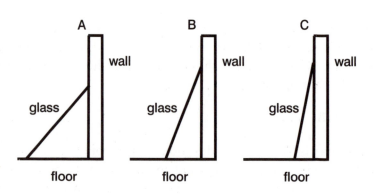

A square piece of glass is temporarily placed upon the floor and leant against a wall. Would it be most safely placed in position A, B or C?

a) A   b) B   c) C   d) does not matter

3.

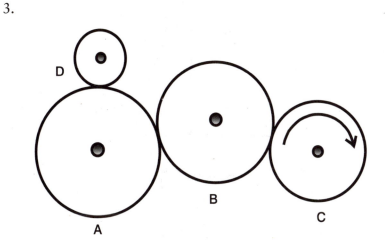

Four rubber wheels, A, B, C and D are touching so that if one moves the others must also move. If wheel C turns in the direction shown, which way will wheel D turn?

a) clockwise   b) all turn the same way   c) anti-clockwise
d) none will turn

4.

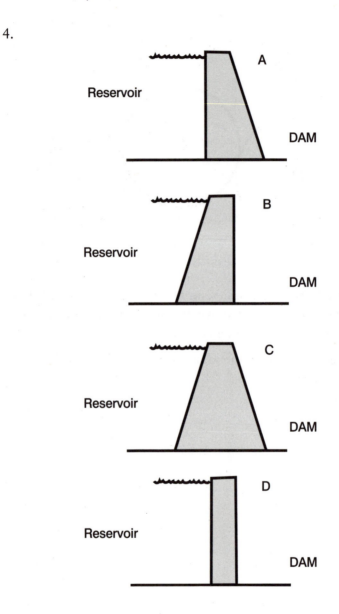

Four designs for a new dam are shown in section above. Which would be the strongest dam?

a) A   b) B   c) C   d) D

5.

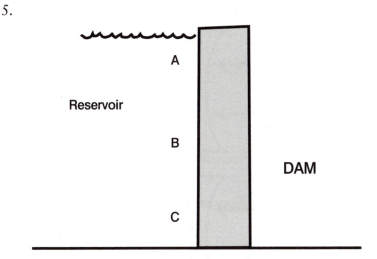

In the design for a new dam shown in section above, at which point does the water exert the greatest pressure?

a) A   b) B   c) C   d) all points equally

6.

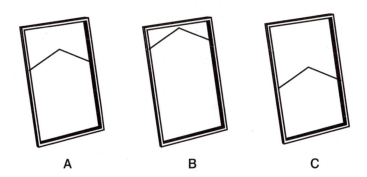

A, B and C are the backs of three picture frames. These are to be hung from a picture hook on a wall by means of a string attached to each side of the back of the frame. Which picture will be flattest against the wall when it is hung?

a) A   b) B   c) C   d) all equally

7.

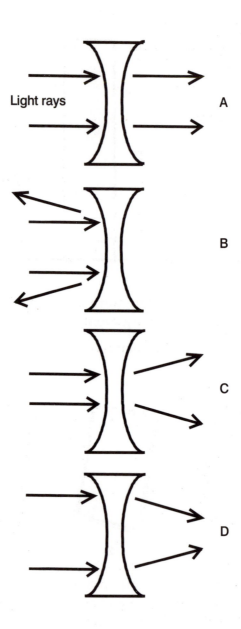

Rays of light strike a concave lens. Which diagram, A, B, C or D most correctly shows how the light rays continue after strking the lens?

a) A   b) B   c) C   d) D

8.

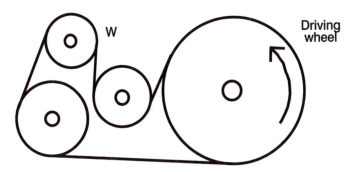

A band passes around all the wheels so that they can all be turned by the driving wheel. When the driving wheel turns in the direction shown, which way does wheel W turn?

a) clockwise   b) cannot move   c) anti-clockwise   d) either way

9.

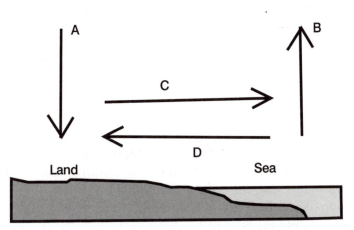

The drawing shows a cross-section where the land meets the sea. The section covered is 5 kilometres. On a hot day, in which direction, indicated by the four arrows, A, B, C or D, is the wind most likely to blow?

a) A   downwards on to the land
b) B   up into the air from the sea
c) C   from the land to the sea
d) D   from the sea to the land

10.

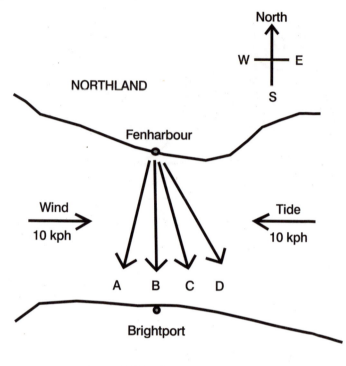

The distance from Fenharbour to Brightport across the channel is 10 kilometres. A sailing boat can do this crossing in an hour. On this particular day, the wind and tide conditions are as given on the map. As the boat leaves Fenharbour, in which direction, A, B, C or D, should the boat be headed in order to make the quickest crossing to Brightport?

a) A   b) B   c) C   d) D

11.

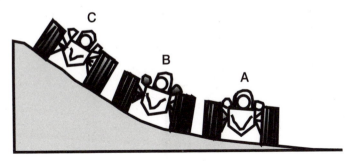

Three racing cars travel exactly alongside each other as they go round the curve of a racing track which has been raised up into a bank. Which car is travelling fastest?

a) A   b) B   c) C   d) all the same

12.

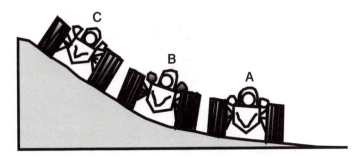

As they went into a left-hand bend, the position of the cars was: first car C, second car B, third car A. As they emerge from the bend, all the cars are level. Which car has travelled at the fastest speed around the bend?

a) A   b) B   c) C   d) cannot say

13.

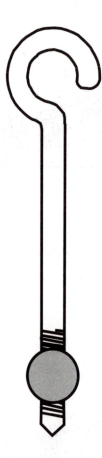

This old-fashioned 'grandfather clock' pendulum and weight are made of iron. They have been taken out of the clock for adjustment, as the clock is running late. To keep correct time, where might the weight need to be adjusted?

a) will not need adjustment   b) upwards   c) downwards

14.

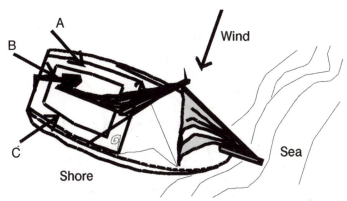

The diagram looks down upon a three-metre dinghy which is about to be launched. In the diagram the sails have not yet been raised and the foresail is flapping in the wind which is blowing from the left-hand side (port). When the dinghy is launched, where should the sailor position herself?

a) A On the left (port)
b) B As near as possible at the back near the tiller
c) C On the right-hand side (starboard)
d) makes no difference

15.

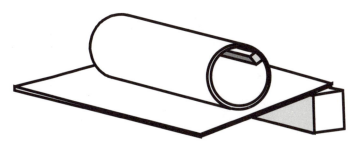

A heavy metal bar is fixed inside a cardboard tube. When the tube is placed on the ramp, as shown, in which direction will the tube roll?

a) down the slope
b) up the slope
c) stay still

16.

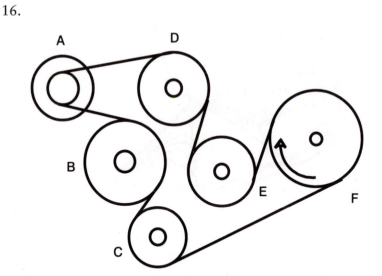

When F turns in the direction shown, which way does A turn?

a) anti-clockwise
b) clockwise
c) system jams

17.

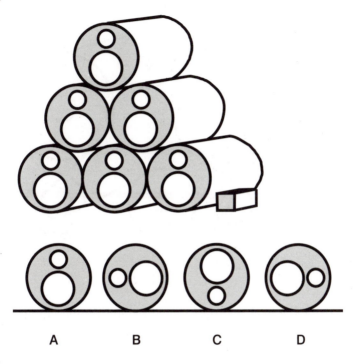

A   B   C   D

Steel cylinders are made so that each one has a large and small hole through the middle. In the drawing, six cylinders have been stacked on top of each other. To stop the cylinders from rolling on the smooth floor, they are wedged by heavy blocks at each side of the bottom row.

If the heavy blocks were removed, what would be the position of each of the cylinders, A, B, C or D, when they stop rolling?

a) A
b) B
c) C
d) D

18.

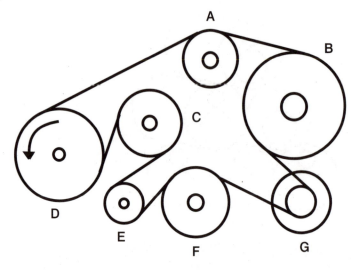

As the driving wheel D turns in the direction shown, and the belt turns the other wheels around, which wheel turns round the most times?

a) A
b) B
c) C
d) D
e) E
f) F
g) G

19.

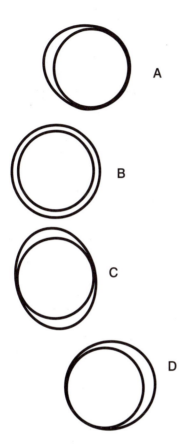

A

B

Moon

C

D

The earth is shown in four different positions in relation to the moon. The earth is covered by water. Which of the four diagrams, A, B, C or D best shows the tidal movement in relation to the earth's position to the moon?

a) A
b) B
c) C
d) D
e) cannot tell

20.

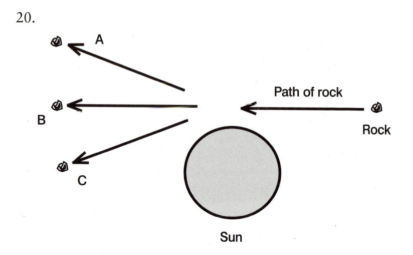

A large lump of rock is travelling through space in a direction that will take it close by the sun before it continues on its way. What is its most likely direction after it has passed by the sun?

a) A
b) B
c) C
d) cannot tell

21.

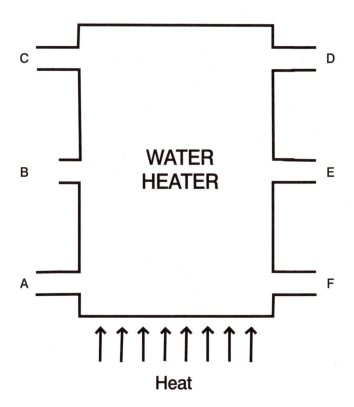

The diagram shows a section through a hot water boiler. As water is heated, the hot water is drawn off through the outlet at D. From which pipe, A, B, C, E, or F should cold water be introduced into the system?

a) A
b) B
c) C
d) does not matter
e) E
f) F

22.

A car, which has no brakes and is not in gear, is easily pushed on to a horizontal ramp. Its rear wheels are then raised as shown. The car is supported only by its free moving wheels.

In this position, with the brake off and not in gear, is it likely to

a) roll forwards?
b) roll backwards?
c) stay in the same position?

23.

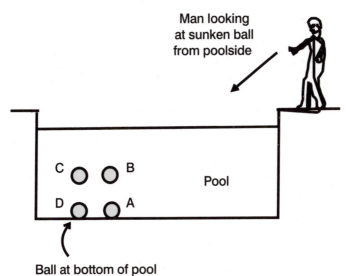

Man looking
at sunken ball
from poolside

Pool

C ○ ○ B

D ○ ○ A

Ball at bottom of pool

A ball sinks to the bottom of a pool and comes to rest at D. What appears to be the position of the ball as viewed by the man at the poolside?

a) at A
b) at B
c) at C

24.

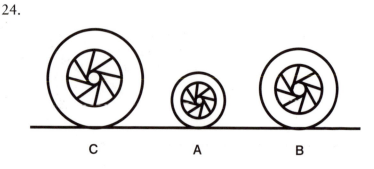

The three wheels all rotate at the speed of one revolution per second. A is the lightest wheel, B is the next heaviest and C is the heaviest. If four wheels of each size were attached to a car, which car, with tyre sizes A, B or C, will win a 1 kilometre race?

a) A
b) B
c) C
d) all equally fast

25.

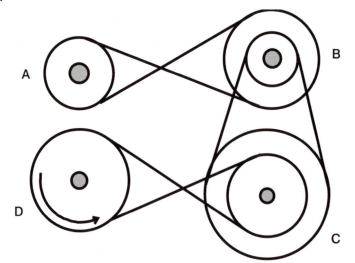

When D turns in the direction shown, which way does A turn?

a) clockwise
b) anti-clockwise
c) system jams

26.

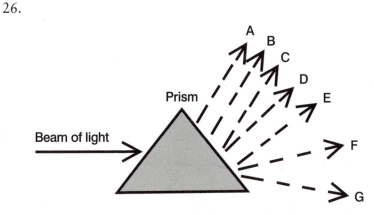

A prism may be used to break up light into its primary colours

A beam of light hits the clear glass prism at the point shown. At which point and in what direction is the light most likely to come out from the prism?

a) A   d) D   g) G

b) B   e) E   h) all of these

c) C   f) F   i) none of these

27.

A   B

Two glass coffee cups contain equal amounts of hot coffee. Which one, A or B, will be the slower to cool?

a) A

b) B

c) both equally

28.

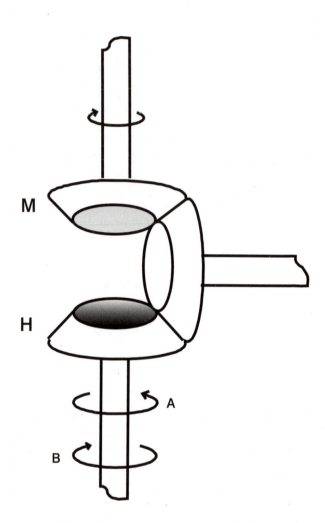

Which way will hellical gear H turn when hellical gear M turns as shown?

a) A
b) B
c) not possible to tell

Marking the test of physical analysis

1 – b	2 – c	3 – c	4 – c	5 – c	6 – b
7 – c	8 – c	9 – d	10 – c	11 – c	12 – d
13 – b	14 – a	15 – b	16 – b	17 – c	18 – g
19 – d	20 – c	21 – a	22 – c	23 – a	24 – c
25 – b	26 – h	27 – b	28 – a		

Number correct = _____ + (2 if there were no mistakes)

= _____ Total score

Score

no evidence	some evidence	good evidence	excellent evidence
IQ range up to 100	IQ range 101–114	IQ range 115–124	IQ range 125+
1–5	6–10	11–15	16+

Interpretation

This test demands a comprehension of what actually happens and what actually works in the real world. Although it is possible to learn the answers to these problems, people with a natural aptitude do well even though they have never seen problems like these before.

It is quite a demanding test, because it also requires you to make sense of the verbal instructions before you start. It is analytical because there are often a number of forces operating within the problems at any one time. You are literally required to 'weigh things in the balance'.

Unfortunately, the fact that you can do well on this test does not always go hand in hand with the practical ability to repair or make things. It usually does, but without the necessary manual dexterity, your ability on this test will be of most use in understanding conceptual and design problems, as opposed to working upon them yourself.

An aptitude to apprehend what is happening in a physical situation and make judgements about what to do is useful in areas of work connected with engineering, but also in many situations where realistic decisions have to be made, often outdoors or in situations of possible danger.

Verbal penetration

This test is to see how you reason with words. For each question there are alternative answers. Mark your choice with a tick against the letter.

Examples
1. Dog is to Pup as Sheep is to
   a) Sheep b) Goat c) Lamb d) Flock

Answer: c)

Explanation for other answers: the answer you have made is not the young of sheep.

2. Vagabond has a similar meaning to
   a) Hobo b) Criminal c) Needy d) Desperate

Answer: a)

Explanation for other answers: the answer you have made is not the best because the word you selected does not describe a person who drifts or wanders. Try again.

3. Glum is the opposite of
   a) Dreamy b) Shadowy c) Cheerful d) Boring

Answer: c)

Explanation for other answers: the answer you gave is not correct. You should find a word which is opposite of glum, gloomy, dull, colourless or dreary. Try again.

Now you can start the test which begins below. You have 10 minutes to do as much as you can. You must work accurately and quickly. Begin as soon as you are ready.

1. Pebble is to Beach as Tree is to
   a) Forest b) Shore c) Hedge d) Garden

2. Prompt is the opposite of
   a) Dull b) Slow c) Miss d) Reject

3. Pig is to Bacon as Sheep is to
   a) Eggs b) Meat c) Mutton d) Animal

4. Which word is closest in meaning to Chip?
   a) Fragment b) Potato c) Wood d) Shoulder

5. Dawn is to Noon as Dusk is to
   a) Night b) Midnight c) Dark d) Afternoon

6. Dog is to Hair as Fish is to
   a) Scales b) Feathers c) Tail d) Fins

7. What means the same as Tail?
   a) Animal b) Follow c) Traffic d) Plane

8. Sock is to Foot as Glove is to
   a) Cover b) Fingers c) Hand d) Pocket

9. What does Blunt mean?
   a) Wooden b) Big c) Pointed d) Outspoken

10. Disloyal is to True as Disagreeable is to
    a) Pleasant b) Steadfast c) Cheer d) Qualify

11. Which is the odd one out?
    a) Democrat b) Communist c) Liberal d) Autocrat

12. Cat is to Paw as Horse is to
    a) Fur b) Hair c) Shoe d) Hoof

13. Exhaust is the opposite of
    a) Clean b) Burn c) Motion d) Liven

14. What does Prodigal mean?
    a) Son b) Excess c) Moderate d) Tempted

15. Which would be third in alphabetical order?
    a) Maundy b) Mauve c) Mausoleum d) Mane

16. Descend is to Ascent as Scale is to
    a) Clamber b) Descent c) Peak d) Level

17. Which is the odd one out?
    a) Profuse b) Abundant c) Lush d) Title

18. Snow is to Crystals as Steam is to
    a) Vapour b) Water c) Cloud d) Rain

19. Which is the odd one out?
    a) Peeved b) Snappy c) Pettish d) Sunny

20. Which is closest in meaning to Humour?
    a) Inflated b) Thwart c) Coax d) Beg

21. What is the opposite of Sparse?
    a) Thin b) Abundant c) Poor d) Build

22. Ignite is to Combustion as Trigger is to
    a) Projectile b) Reaction c) Gun d) War

23. Boost is to Degrade as Applaud is to
    a) Anger b) Submit c) Humiliate d) Defer

24. Oblivious is the opposite of
    a) Uncontrollable b) Impecunious c) Observant d) Poor

25. Which is the odd one out?
    a) Disgrace b) Affront c) Honour d) Abuse

26. Rock is to Geology as Seed is to
    a) Horticulture b) Biology c) Atom d) Science

27. Which is the odd one out?
    a) Concurrent b) Mutual c) Unison d) Independent

28. Stanza is to Poem as Movement is to
    a) Symphony b) Race c) Music d) Dance

29. What does Plosive mean?
    a) Breath b) Possible c) Imminent d) Dynamite

30. Chivvy is to Chase as Seek is to
    a) Hide b) Inquire c) Deny d) Flee

31. Bird is to Flock as Subject is to
    a) Populace b) Story c) Object d) Matter

32. Stock is the opposite of
    a) Common b) Frequent c) Standard d) Unusual

33. Donor is to Philanthropist as Recipient is to
    a) Patient b) Collector c) Legatee d) Giver

34. Which is the odd one out?
   a) Enervated b) Potent c) Energetic d) Lively

35. Which is the odd one out?
   a) Momentary b) Fleeting c) Situation d) Ephemeral

36. Sanguine is to Ruddy as Scent is to
   a) Fresh b) Aseptic c) Pallid d) Aroma

37. Sap is the opposite of
   a) Brace b) Dilute c) Mine d) Debilitate

38. Which is the odd one out?
   a) Spirited b) Quenched c) Brisk d) Spry

39. Which is the odd one out?
   a) Inferior b) Cheap c) Shoddy d) Rare

40. Impulsive is to Deliberate as Impetuous is to
   a) Reflective b) Assist c) Decelerate d) Hasty

41. Retard is to Impel as Obfuscate is to
   a) Hallucinate b) Confuse c) Irradiate d) Dampen

42. Which is the odd one out?
   a) Kind b) Ilk c) Furnish d) Stock

Marking the test of verbal penetration

1 – a	2 – b	3 – c	4 – a	5 – b	6 – a
7 – b	8 – c	9 – d	10 – a	11 – d	12 – d
13 – d	14 – b	15 – c	16 – b	17 – d	18 – a
19 – d	20 – c	21 – b	22 – b	23 – c	24 – c
25 – c	26 – b	27 – d	28 – a	29 – a	30 – b
31 – a	32 – d	33 – c	34 – a	35 – c	36 – d
37 – a	38 – b	39 – d	40 – a	41 – c	42 – c

Number correct = _____ + (3 if there were no mistakes) = ____
Add a further 3 marks if you are aged under 18 = _____ Total
score

Score

no evidence	some evidence	good evidence	excellent evidence
IQ range up to 100	IQ range 101–114	IQ range 115–124	IQ range 125+
1–11	12–20	21–28	29+

Interpretation

To perform well on this test, it is necessary to have a very good level of vocabulary in order to understand fine distinctions between different concepts. Therefore, without an existing level of ability, your aptitude may not appear. It is an aptitude that can be developed with learning. The test of critical dissection, which appears later on, is less dependent upon vocabulary.

The test of verbal penetration asks you to make distinctions between words that have similar meanings. Sometimes the distinctions are very fine indeed, so that you have to be able to grasp the idea that is represented by the word. As there are rarely two words which have exactly the same meaning, what is wanted is often inexact. Therefore, this test shows how well you can resolve ambiguities in language. It establishes how well you can discover the 'thread' which is buried in hidden meanings.

This aptitude is useful in areas of work where words are used in analysis and in precision of communication. Literary careers would demand this aptitude, as would legal work, administration and areas connected with communications.

Numerical deduction

This tests how easily you think with numbers.

You are given a series of numbers. Your task is to see how they go together to form a relationship with each other. You then have to choose the number which would go next in the series, choosing from the four possible answers provided.

It is advisable to have a piece of scrap paper and a pencil to do any working out that may be necessary. Mark the correct answer with a tick.

Examples
1.   2   4   6   8   10   ?   a) 11 b) 20 c) 12 d) 18
Answer: c)
Explanation: the numbers are a series. The next one in the series should be 2 more.

2.   14   12.5 11 9.5 8   ?   a) 6.5 b) 5.5 c) 7.5 d) 6
Answer: a)
Explanation: the series is reducing by 1.5, so you should take 1.5 away from 8.

3.   1   3   7   15   31   ?   a) 46 b) 62 c) 61 d) 63
Answer: d)
Explanation: the gaps between the numbers are 2, 4, 8 and 16, so what number would fill the gap between the last and the missing number? Alternatively, this series can be done by doubling each of the numbers in the series and adding 1.

You have 10 minutes to do as much as you can. You must work as quickly and as accurately as you can. Remember, you are likely to need a piece of scrap paper and a pencil. Begin as soon as you are ready.

1. 0 5 10 15 20 ? a) 20 b) 25 c) 30 d) 21

2. .25 .5 1 2 4 ? a) 12 b) 16 c) 8 d) 10

3. 98 50 26 14 8 ? a) 4 b) 2 c) 6 d) 5

4. 1 2 3 5 8 ? a) 5 b) 11 c) 8 d) 13

5. 4 8 12 16 20 ? a) 25 b) 22 c) 24 d) 28

6. 160 120 100 90 85 ? a) 78.5 b) 80 c) 82.5 d) 84

7. .55 .65 .75 .85 .95 ? a) 1.05 b) 1.5 c) 1.15 d) 9.5

8. 1 3 8 19 42 ? a) 84 b) 89 c) 71 d) 85

9. 2 7 12 17 22 ? a) 26 b) 28 c) 23 d) 27

10. 1 7 13 19 25 ? a) 18 b) 15 c) 31 d) 33

11. 3 8 22 63 185 ? a) 550 b) 270 c) 365 d) 248

12. 7 7 9 13 19 ? a) 25 b) 29 c) 31 d) 27

13. 1 1 2 4 7 ? a) 6 b) 11 c) 8 d) 12

14. 0 –1 0 3 8 ? a) 15 b) 11 c) 12 d) 24

15. 0 3 3 6 9 ? a) 12 b) 15 c) 18 d) 9

16. 6 9 3 8 3 ? a) 7 b) 6 c) 8 d) 10

17. 7 12 9 19 13 ? a) 22 b) 30 c) 32 d) 28

18. 75 50 90 65 105 ? a) 185 b) 130 c) 80 d) 170

19. 3 9 4 16 11 ? a) 27 b) 44 c) 25 d) 35

20. 17 11 28 39 67 ? a) 96 b) 106 c) 95 d) 58

21. 5 3 4 9 23 ? a) 41 b) 60 c) 34 d) 32

Marking the test of numerical deduction

1 – b	2 – c	3 – d	4 – d	5 – c	6 – c
7 – a	8 – b	9 – d	10 – c	11 – a	12 – d
13 – b	14 – a	15 – b	16 – d	17 – d	18 – c
19 – d	20 – b	21 – b			

Number correct = _____ + (2 if there were no mistakes)
= _____ Total score

Score

no evidence	some evidence	good evidence	excellent evidence
IQ range up to 100	IQ range 101–114	IQ range 115–124	IQ range 125+
1–4	5–7	8–11	12+

Interpretation

To perform well on this test, you have to perceive how numbers relate to each other. As you will have realized, it is more than a test of arithmetic. In fact, many people who think that they are 'terrible' at arithmetic often surprise themselves by doing better on this test than they expect.

Each series of numbers is like a code which contains a hidden message. You have to work out the relationship of the numbers with each other to deduce the answer. It is a logical exercise, without the subtleties of interpretation needed in the test of verbal penetration.

The aptitude for discovering the logic in a series of pieces of connected information is essential in many areas of work. These are often the mathematical sciences where quantification and precise technical information exchange are required. This aptitude is found in statistically-based commercial activities as well as most highly technical and research-based ones.

Observation

This test looks at how easily you can reason with signs and shapes.

After each question there are four possible answers. Only one is correct. Tick the answer you think is the correct one.

Examples

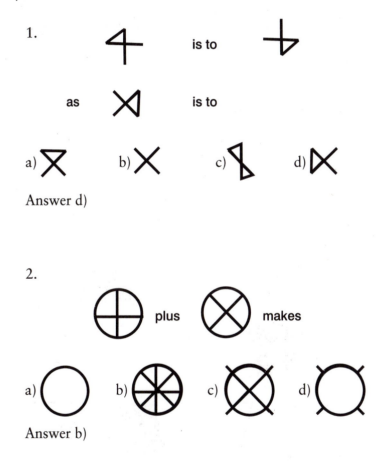

1.

4   is to   ⅄

as   ⋈   is to

a) ⅄   b) ✕   c) ⅄   d) ⋈

Answer d)

2.

⊕ plus ⊗ makes

a) ○   b) ✳   c) ⊗   d) ○

Answer b)

3. Which comes next?

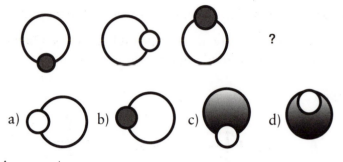

Answer a)

In the test you have 10 minutes to do as many as you can. Begin as soon as you are ready

1.

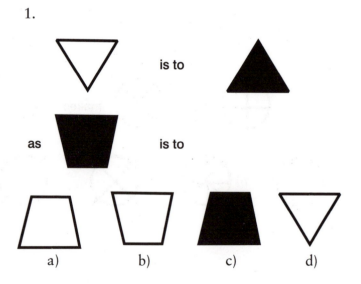

2. Which comes next?

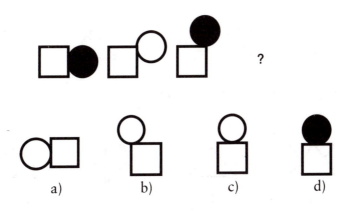

a)   b)   c)   d)

3. Which is the odd one out?

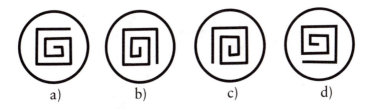

a)   b)   c)   d)

4.

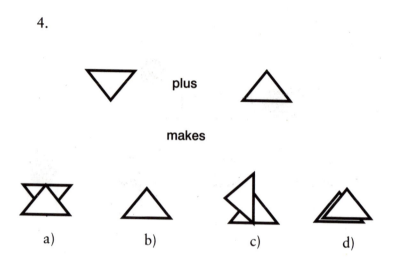

a)   b)   c)   d)

5. Which comes next?

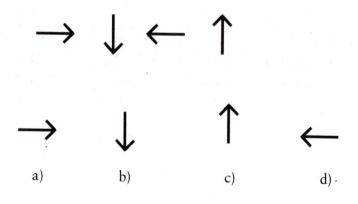

a)   b)   c)   d) .

6.

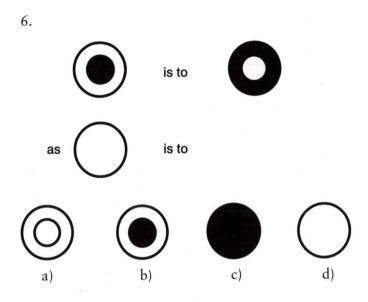

a)   b)   c)   d)

7.

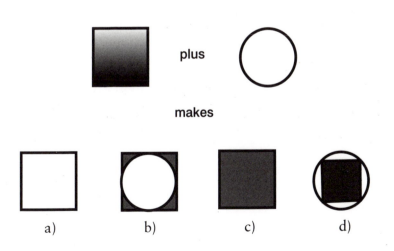

a)   b)   c)   d)

8. Which comes next?

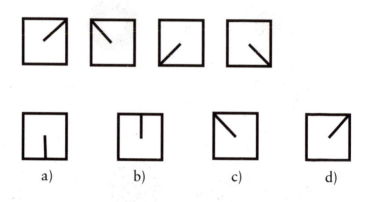

a)   b)   c)   d)

9. Which is the odd one out?

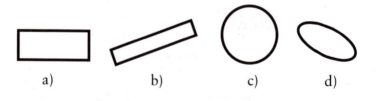

a)   b)   c)   d)

10.

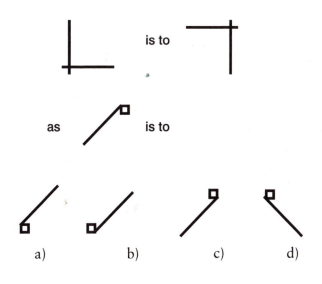

a)   b)   c)   d)

11.

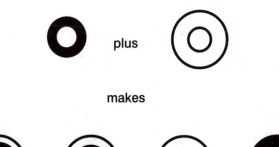

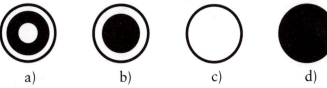

a)   b)   c)   d)

12. Which is the odd one out?

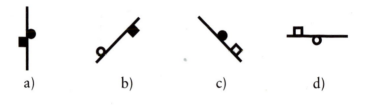

a)   b)   c)   d)

13. Which comes next?

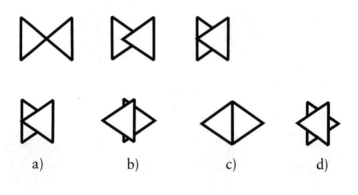

a)   b)   c)   d)

14.

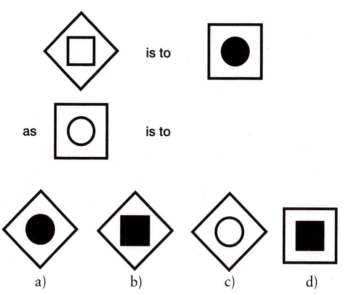

is to

as   is to

a)   b)   c)   d)

15. Which is the odd one out?

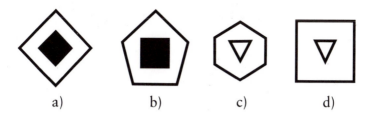

a)   b)   c)   d)

16. Which comes next?

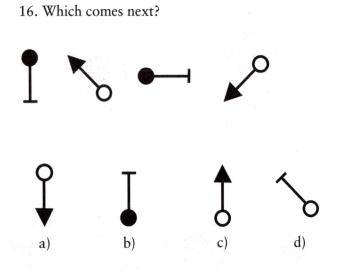

17.

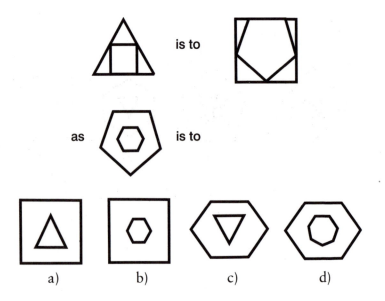

18. Which comes next?

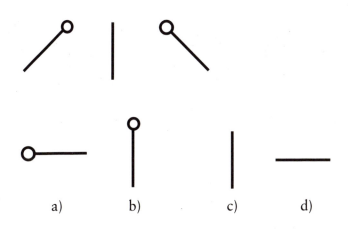

a)   b)   c)   d)

19.

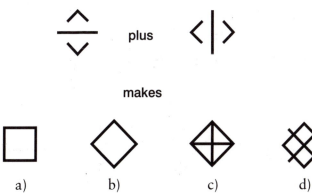

plus

makes

a)   b)   c)   d)

20. Which is the odd one out?

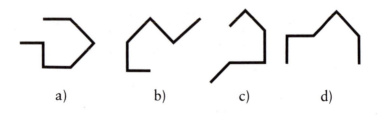

a)   b)   c)   d)

21. Which comes next?

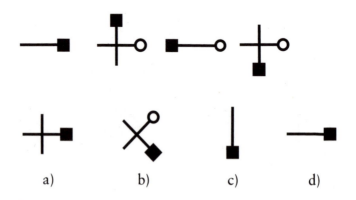

a)   b)   c)   d)

22.

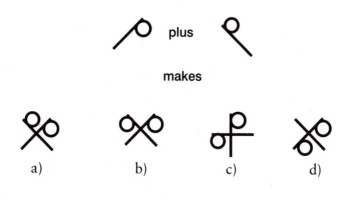

plus

makes

a)   b)   c)   d)

23. Which is the odd one out?

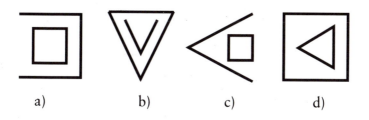

a)   b)   c)   d)

24.

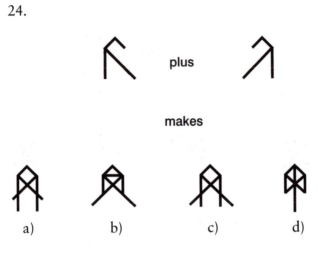

plus

makes

a)   b)   c)   d)

25.

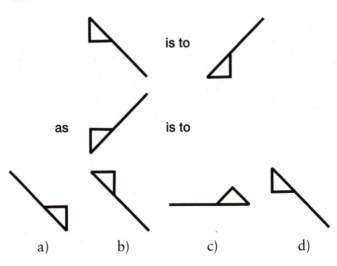

is to

as   is to

a)   b)   c)   d)

26. Which comes next?

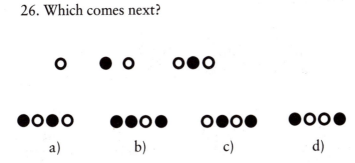

a) b) c) d)

27.

 plus

makes

a) b) c) d)

28. Which comes next?

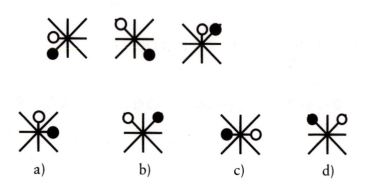

a)   b)   c)   d)

29. Which comes next?

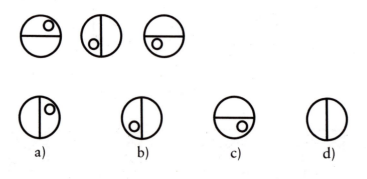

a)   b)   c)   d)

30. Which is the odd one out?

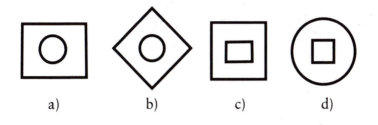

a)   b)   c)   d)

31. Which comes next?

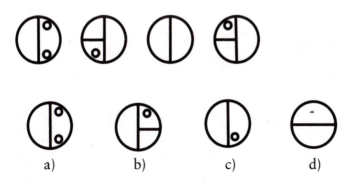

a)   b)   c)   d)

32.

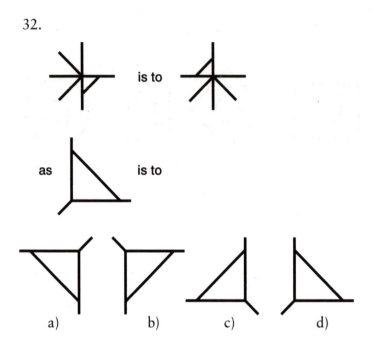

is to

as   is to

a)   b)   c)   d)

33. Which comes next?

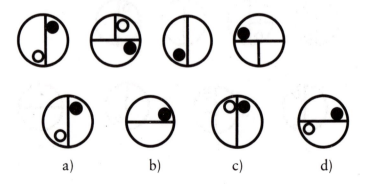

a)   b)   c)   d)

34. Which is the odd one out?

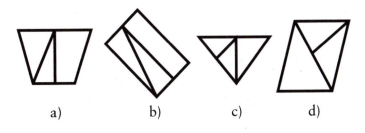

a)   b)   c)   d)

35. Which comes next?

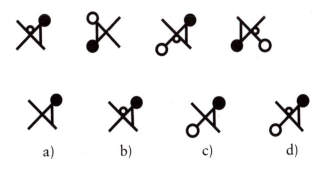

a)   b)   c)   d)

Marking the test of observation

1 – a	2 – c	3 – c	4 – a	5 – a	6 – c
7 – b	8 – d	9 – c	10 – b	11 – a	12 – c
13 – d	14 – b	15 – a	16 – b	17 – d	18 – c
19 – c	20 – a	21 – d	22 – a	23 – d	24 – c
25 – b	26 – a	27 – c	28 – d	29 – a	30 – c
31 – a	32 – d	33 – a	34 – d	35 – b	

Number correct = _____ + (3 if there were no mistakes) = _____
Total score

Score

no evidence	some evidence	good evidence	excellent evidence
IQ range up to 100	IQ range 101–114	IQ range 115–124	IQ range 125+
1–12	13–17	18–22	23+

Interpretation

This is a logical reasoning test without the use of words or numbers. You are required to collect information visually in order to project what would happen next in the series.

This aptitude demands that details, together with their relevance to the whole picture, are perceived clearly. It is a necessary aptitude in many sciences and in many areas where information is researched and essential details need to be abstracted.

Critical dissection

In this test you are asked to draw logical conclusions from the information you have been given. There is always enough information for you to come to the correct conclusion. You should not draw upon any previous experience or information as this is not likely to help you.

Because of the amount of information you are sometimes asked to deal with, it is recommended that you have a piece of scrap paper so that you can, if you wish, draw diagrams or make notes.

Examples
Following some facts are some alternative answers. Tick the answer you think is correct.

1. Mary is heavier than Jane. Joan is heavier than Mary.
    Who is lightest?   a) Joan b) Mary c) Jane

Answer: c)
Cannot be a) because Joan is heavier than Mary.
Cannot be b) because Mary is heavier than Jane.

2. Fred, Cindy and Sue all have two pet animals each. One of them does not have a dog. Cindy is the only one to have a cat. Sue has a dog. Fred and Cindy have hamsters.
    Who has a tortoise?   a) Fred b) Cindy c) Sue

Answer: c)
Cannot be a). Fred has a hamster and a dog.
Cannot be b). Cindy has a cat and a hamster.

You have 15 minutes to do as much of the test as you can. Get your scrap paper and pencil ready in case you need them. Work as accurately and as fast as you can. When you are ready, start the clock and begin.

1. Mr Brown lives to the west of Mr Smith. Mr Burton lives to the west of Mr Brown.
    Who lives furthest west?   a) Mr Brown b) Mr Smith c) Mr Burton

2. Susan and Stella like pizza, but Sukie and Sally like pasta. Susan and Sally both like lasagne.
    Who likes pizza and lasagne?
    a) Susan b) Stella c) Sukie d) Sally

3. Who likes lasagne and pasta?
    a) Susan b) Stella c) Sukie d) Sally

4. Joan and Jack have more money to spend than Fred, although Chris has less than Fred. Peter has more money to spend than Fred.
    Who has the least to spend?
    a) Joan b) Jack c) Fred d) Chris e) Peter

5. Toby, Rob and Frank all take a packed lunch to work, while Sam, Jo and Tony buy a meal in the canteen. Frank, Sam and Jo travel by bus. Jo, Rob and Tony are married.
    Who is married and has a packed lunch?
    a) Toby b) Rob c) Frank d) Sam e) Jo f) Tony

6. Who does not travel by bus and buys a meal?
    a) Toby b) Rob c) Frank d) Sam e) Jo f) Tony

7. In reverse order of fastest runner over 100 metres, the slowest is Janet, then Marcus, Eric and Angela, who almost loses to him. After training, Janet beats Eric, although Marcus fails to beat him.
    Who is fastest after training?
    a) Janet b) Marcus c) Eric d) Angela

8. Who comes last after training?
   a) Janet b) Marcus c) Eric d) Angela

9. Fred, John, Garth and Joe all have similar jobs although Fred and John are the only ones who have full-time work, the others working on a part-time basis. John and Joe travel to work by train, while the distance to work is short enough for the others to walk. Only Fred and Joe own cars.
   Who owns a car, but goes to work by train?
   a) Fred b) Joe c) John d) Garth

10. Who does not own a car and travels to their full-time job by train?   a) Fred b) Joe c) Garth d) John

11. In a bookcase, a copy of *The Winter's Tale* is to be found underneath the shelf on which is found *The Horse's Mouth*. *The Last Days of the Third Reich* is on the shelf above *A Book of Practical Cats*. On the top shelf is *The Wind in the Willows*. *The Horse's Mouth* is on the same shelf as *Justine*, whereas *A Book of Practical Cats* is on the shelf below *A Winter's Tale*.
    Which book is on the bottom shelf?
    a) *The Winter's Tale* b) *The Horse's Mouth* c) *The Last Days of the Third Reich* d) *A Book of Practical Cats* e) *Justine* f) *The Wind in the Willows*

12. Which two books are on the same shelf?
    a) *The Winter's Tale* and *The Last Days of the Third Reich* b) *The Horse's Mouth* and *A Book of Practical Cats* c) *A Book of Practical Cats* and *The Wind in the Willows* d) none of these

13. Casey, Stuart, Ritchie, Billie and Colin all have their own desk at school. Casey and Colin have computers on their desks, while the others have calculators. Ritchie and Casey have a manual as well as an instruction sheet. The others only have instruction sheets. Casey and Billie have desks made of wood. The others have metal ones.
Who has a computer on a wooden desk?
a) Casey b) Stuart c) Ritchie d) Billie e) Colin

14. How many people have instruction sheets on non-metal desks and do not have a computer?
a) 5 b) 4 c) 3 d) 2 e) 1 f) none

15. Who does not have a computer on their metal desk, but has a manual as well as an instruction sheet?
a) Casey b) Stuart c) Ritchie d) Billie e) Colin

16. Mrs Howard has difficulty feeding her four children as each one will only eat certain foods. Kelly and Sam both eat corn and beans. Sharon and Robina will eat fish and tomatoes. Kelly and Sharon are the only ones who like potatoes and corn.
Which is the only food that Sharon does not eat?
a) corn b) beans c) fish d) tomatoes e) potatoes

17. Who eats potatoes, corn and beans?
a) Sharon b) Kelly c) Robina d) Sam

18. Who eats fish and tomatoes, but doesn't eat potatoes?
a) Sharon b) Kelly c) Robina d) Sam

19. Which food will be acceptable to most of the children?
a) corn b) beans c) fish d) tomatoes e) potatoes

20. There are five cars belonging to Mr Bagshaw, Miss Jenkins, Mrs Chance, Mr Fleming, and Mr Marx. Mr Marx's and Mr Bagshaw's cars are blue. The others have red ones. Mr Bagshaw and Mrs Chance have a white stripe on the sides of

their cars which matches their upholstery. Miss Jenkins has a blue stripe on the side of her car. Mr Fleming's and Mr Marx's cars have orange stripes. The upholstery of all the cars is white apart for Miss Jenkins's and Mr Fleming's which are blue.
Who has a car with blue upholstery and an orange stripe?
a) Mr Bagshaw b) Miss Jenkins c) Mrs Chance d) Mr Fleming e) Mr Marx

21. Who has a car with an orange stripe and white upholstery?
a) Mr Bagshaw b) Miss Jenkins c) Mrs Chance d) Mr Fleming e) Mr Marx

22. Who has got the red car with a blue stripe and blue upholstery?
a) Mr Bagshaw b) Miss Jenkins c) Mrs Chance d) Mr Fleming e) Mr Marx

23. Harry the 'Hammer' Quaid, Randy 'Rockjaw' Jones, Simon 'Dodger' Barlow and Manny the 'Merciless' Moorcock are all boxers who compete against each other so that there are six fights in order to decide the champion. Moorcock is beaten by Quaid. Jones beats Moorcock. Quaid and Barlow beat Jones. Barlow beats Quaid and Moorcock.
How many fights does Jones win?   a) 1 b) 2 c) 3 d) 4 e) 0

24. How many fights does Quaid win?   a) 1 b) 2 c) 3 d) 4 e) 0

25. Who emerges as the champion?
a) Quaid b) Jones c) Barlow d) Moorcock

26. Sally, Cheryl, Laura, Tom and Sandy help themselves to some sweets from a bowl. Four of them each take a piece of fudge. Cheryl and Tom do not take a piece of chocolate as all the others do. In fact, Cheryl takes only one sweet, which is a fruit gum. Apart from Cheryl, only Sally and Sandy do not take a piece of toffee.
Who only had a piece of toffee and a piece of fudge?
a) Sally b) Cheryl c) Laura d) Tom e) Sandy

27. Who had three sweets?
    a) Sally b) Cheryl c) Laura d) Tom e) Sandy

28. Who are the two people who took the same number and type of sweets?
    a) Sally and Cheryl b) Cheryl and Laura c) Laura and Tom d) Tom and Sandy e) Sandy and Sally

29. In total, how many sweets were taken by the group?
    a) 7 b) 8 c) 9 d) 10 e) 11 f) 12

30. John, Rick and Ted are boys who each have a penknife, a key and a book in their pockets. Each penknife is a different weight, being light, fairly heavy and very heavy. The other two objects can be classified in the same way with respect to their weights. Each boy has an object of a different weight, that is, one that is light, one that is fairly heavy and one that is very heavy. The key belonging to Ted is not the fairly heavy one. Rick's book and John's penknife are the same weight. Ted's book, Rick's penknife and John's key can all be described the same way as regards their weight. Ted's penknife is a very heavy one.
    What weight is Ted's key?
    a) light b) fairly heavy c) very heavy

31. What weight is John's book?
    a) light b) fairly heavy c) very heavy

32. Which boy has the fairly heavy key?
    a) John b) Rick c) Ted

33. Which boy has the light book?
    a) John b) Rick c) Ted

Marking the test of critical dissection

1 – c	2 – a	3 – d	4 – d	5 – b	6 – f
7 – d	8 – b	9 – b	10 – d	11 – d	12 – a
13 – a	14 – e	15 – c	16 – b	17 – b	18 – c
19 – a	20 – d	21 – e	22 – b	23 – a	24 – b
25 – c	26 – d	27 – c	28 – e	29 – d	30 – a
31 – c	32 – a	33 – b			

Number correct = _____ + (3 if there were no mistakes)

= _____ Total score

Score

no evidence	some evidence	good evidence	excellent evidence
IQ range up to 100	IQ range 101–114	IQ range 115–124	IQ range 125+
1–7	8–13	14–17	18+

Interpretation

This test requires careful analysis of the information given. Often you are required to 'fill in' missing information, which you must detect from the fragments you have been given. The items in the test are puzzles that require persistence and power of concentration.

If you can do this test, you will be able to succeed in many areas of work which require a sensible approach to problem solving in which you do not allow yourself to be distracted by irrelevant information, and where you do not allow yourself to become influenced by emotions. These may be situations which involve people and their problems, as well as technically specialist areas.

Interpreting your profile

Below you will find a large chart entitled 'Your aptitude profile'. Place your own scores in the chart by circling your own score in the appropriate place.

If you connect up the scores, you should have a graph which looks something like this:

Example profile

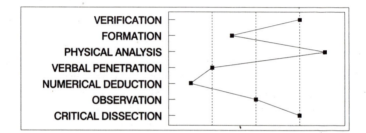

Your profile readily enables you to see possible differences between your scores. These differences may not be significant. For example, on another occasion the differences between scores might be reversed, so that on one occasion you seem to do better with observation than verification, but on the next occasion do better with verification than observation. This may be because you are really equally good on both tests. It may be that tiredness, or other reasons, affect your performance on different occasions.

However, the greater the difference between tests, the more likely it is that you really are better on one type of test than another. This difference may be important to you in determining the most suitable area of study or what career to pursue.

Read the following if your test scores are different from what you had assumed and if you disagree with the results. If you wish, there is no reason why you should not place your own estimates of your potential, if these are different from your test results, in the chart. It depends how strongly you feel that the test results are not fully and accurately assessing you. There is always room for some doubt. As I have said, your results on the tests might be affected by all sorts of issues relating to a) the efficiency with which you test yourself, b) the conditions in which you test yourself, c) who you compare yourself with, and d) whether the tests themselves have reliably detected your potential. Therefore, your own estimates might be based upon your progress at school and upon other experiences.

Your aptitude profile

Test	no evidence IQ range up to 100		some evidence IQ range 101–114		good evidence IQ range 115–124		strong evidence IQ range 125+	
VERIFICATION	1–4	5–7	8–11	12–15	16–19	20–23	24–27	28+
FORMATION	1–26	27–30	31–34	35–38	39–42	43–46	47–50	51+
PHYSICAL ANALYSIS	1–3	4–5	6–8	9–10	11–12	13–15	16–17	18+
VERBAL PENETRATION	1–7	8–11	12–16	17–20	21–24	25–28	29–32	33+
NUMERICAL DEDUCTION	1–2	3–4	5–6	7	8–9	10–11	12–13	14+
OBSERVATION	1–9	10–12	13–14	15–17	18–19	20–22	23–25	26+
CRITICAL DISSECTION	1–6	7–9	10–11	12–13	14–15	16–17	18–20	21+

(handwritten: 22, 34)

As a rough guide, take it that if there is a clear section (score area) between two scores, then there may be a significant difference in your aptitude. For example, if your score on one test is in the upper section of good evidence and another score is in the upper part of some evidence, there will be a section between the two scores. It then seems possible that your aptitudes really are different on these two tests. The more sections there are between the two scores, the more certain you can be.

How much weight you place upon the difference between any two scores is, in the end, for you to judge.

Interpretation of your profile is reasonably easy if you have one result which stands out from the others. There remains the difficulty of relating this aptitude to a career – even a distinct aptitude may translate into numerous career options – but at least you can be sure of where your major intellectual and practical strength lies. Comments in relation to each test have already been made above.

Most people will obtain a pattern where there is no single, distinguishable aptitude, but rather a pattern which appears to consist of relative 'highs and lows'. Your highest score might be the best indication, but also look at the two highest, the three highest or, even, the four highest.

For example, do your scores seem to group themselves in any way? How are your high scores different from your lower scores? Some people do better with all the word and numerical types of test, but not visual types and practical types. This would be interpreted as more of an administrative as opposed to an artistic pattern. Others may do well on both the numerical and perceptual test, but not so well on the verbal side. This might indicate more of a scientific bias. There are, of course, many possible patterns for you to interpret.

The following are some of the common patterns which can arise. The level of the various scores is not particularly relevant; it is the pattern with which we are concerned. Your own pattern is unlikely to be identical, but may give you some guide as to what your own pattern might mean.

Communications profile

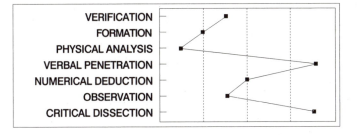

In this pattern, it is the two tests requiring the use of words that are being focused upon. These do not need to be equal, but are likely to be pronounced. The other scores and their levels are less significant, though these may give you some additional help as to how to employ your communications potential most fully.

People who have this type of pattern not only have a sound working knowledge of language in order to express themselves precisely, but they are frequently able to deduce and debate in great depth. These people will make their careers where they are able to use words, for example, journalism or the law, or in many other careers where they might be involved in management. In the latter case, they will be most effective where they are relating to others most of the time, perhaps in sales, but they will be less suited to areas of management which involve them in technical or accounting aspects.

Clerical profile

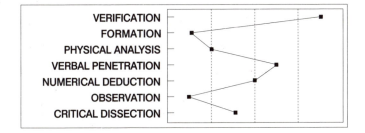

In the clerical profile, the most elevated score is verification, although the verbal and numerical scores might be as high. It is different from the administrative profile, below, where the verbal and numerical scores are at least as high as for verification.

The clerical profile emphasizes dealing with verbal and numerical information with speed and accuracy, but not necessarily using that information for writing or for analysis.

This pattern of aptitude is often found in occupations where attention to detail is required. However, it is not the same sort of potential as is found in technical or scientific occupations. It is found in translators, proof readers, legal occupations and in secretarial areas of work.

Administrative profile

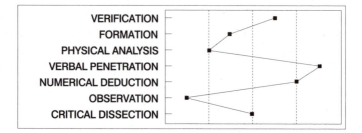

This pattern has about equal potential with words as with numbers. Some people may be stronger in one area than the other.

There is plenty of scope for those who have this type of pattern, these aptitudes being the most generally useful in almost all areas of work. For example, it translates very well into many commercial areas of business, of public service administration, and professional careers such as accounting.

Social profile

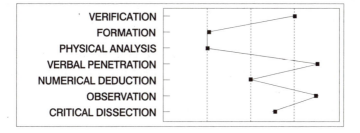

The social profile could also be called the social science profile. It combines an aptitude with words with other, logical reasoning aptitudes.

People who have this pattern often like to acquire information, while also expressing themselves cogently. They may use this creatively, for example, in writing an historical novel, or in some other way in which they become an expert.

Researchers in various fields often have this pattern. It can be found in information scientists and in many areas connected with human sciences, including biology, human geography, history and sociology.

Science profile

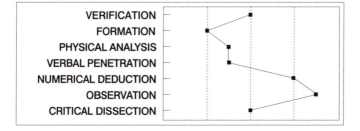

In the science profile, the emphasis has been put upon reasoning with logical, visual information, rather than with words or numbers. Scientists frequently have this bias, although they may be more or less numerical.

However, high numerical aptitude is necessary in most sciences; powers of observation remain necessary for science, but numeracy is vital for many areas of statistical analysis and mathematical modelling. Indeed, a mathematician may well show stronger numerical deduction than observation. Critical dissection might also be shown more strongly than in the example above.

The scientific profile relates to careers where there is investigation and experimentation. Often, this will relate to analytical work in laboratories, or to theoretical work in academic settings. Careers might be in physics, medicine, biology, chemistry, experimental psychology, and so on.

Technological profile

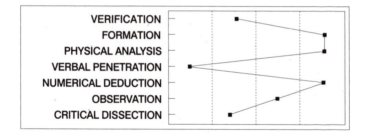

The technological profile requires theoretical aptitudes as well as practical ones. People who have this profile generally want to take theory and apply it in order to accomplish something which works or is useful.

Numerical reasoning is essential for professional engineering, and is also necessary at quite a high level for technical jobs. Thereafter, the bias might be towards the design side, indicated by spatial recognition, or the mechanical side, indicated by physical analysis. One or the other almost always needs to be present.

Sometimes, technologists also obtain higher scores on observation or critical dissection as well.

Careers are in engineering and technology. There are thus many opportunities in civil, mechanical, aeronautical or production engineering. Computer technology and systems engineering are other examples of expanding areas of work.

Design profile

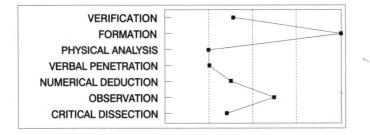

The design profile shows an elevated formation in order to emphasize the sense of form and symmetry required in related careers. These are usually thought of as artistic careers, such as fine art itself. It is found in graphic designers, but because of its 3-D nature, this aptitude is more likely to be found in occupations which are connected with engineering and technology. Packaging design, car design and textile design would be examples. These areas of work usually require other aptitudes as well, particularly numerical ones.

Designers may also score more highly on the test of observation, their visual sense assisting them there. However, they are less scientific than artistic due to their personality and motivation. If formation aptitudes are unaccompanied by pronounced aptitudes in other areas, the more likely they are to lead to strictly artistic careers or to careers related to crafts.

Academic profile

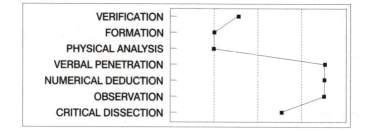

The academic profile rarely shows equal scores on the three tests in the manner shown in the figure. More usually, there is a bias towards reasoning with words, numbers or perceptual logic. This bias then indicates possible leanings towards studies in the arts, humanities or sciences. The score on critical dissection might also be as high as one of the three main scores.

It is usual to find that people with one or more of these aptitudes do well at school. The example shows less emphasis upon other visual and practical aptitudes, though, naturally, there is no reason why these should not also be present in people who do well academically. However, as far as a career is concerned, it is more likely that the academic aptitudes are the ones which would be developed.

Craft profile

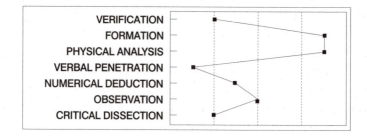

The craft profile emphasizes the practical eye for detail and form that is required in occupations which also have a physical contact with materials and processes. Such occupations are quite the opposite of those that demand verbal and numerical aptitudes in an office setting. Of course, many people who work in crafts may also possess those aptitudes as well, but not be motivated to use them.

Craft careers may be almost artistic. Usually, they combine an artistic sense with some practical sense, for example, in craft pottery, chair making, joinery, thatching, iron working, modelling, and a host of others.

Where the aptitude is more mechanical, careers might also include repair work, or lead to an involvement with machinery and other equipment.

IQ

Your IQ (Intelligence Quotient) is a number by which you can compare yourself with other people. In an indirect way, you have already been doing this with your test results in this book. All that an IQ does is attempt to give you more precise information as to where you stand on the comparative scale.

The reservations I have made already with regard to accuracy in measuring your aptitudes apply to an even greater degree when estimating your IQ. This book cannot measure your IQ with any great accuracy, as the conditions for measuring your IQ, as well as the information required to compare your intelligence with a satisfactory sample of people like you, are not available.

Why, then, provide a guide to IQ? Because many people find the exercise interesting for its own sake. And because the tests in this book are very similar to other tests used to measure intelligence, it enables a fuller comprehension of the entire process of intellectual measurement. Furthermore, an estimate of IQ provides a quick way of asking yourself whether you are going in a direction with your studies or in your career that will allow you to fully use your potential.

Intelligence tests

These are designed to assess innate qualities as far as possible uncontaminated by learning. This is why so many intelligence tests seem to be so abstract and unrelated to what we usually do. In practice, it is very difficult indeed to assess intelligence without using words, figures or shapes that have at least some familiarity to you. The other side to this equation is that the whole point of measuring IQ is to see whether a person has intelligence that has not yet been developed. It thus provides a measure of how much more a person could achieve, if circumstances could be arranged to permit realization of that person's innate potential.

Aptitude tests may be slightly different from intelligence tests, because they are designed to assess potential for something specific. For example, rather that assess to what degree a person may be able to think through problems, aptitude tests attempt to assess whether a person can think through problems which are relevant to distinct fields of endeavour. What distinguishes aptitude tests from intelligence tests is that the purpose of aptitude tests is more practical.

The IQ scale

Most IQ scales use the number 100 as an average. People with above average scores, say, up to about 115 on appropriate tests, usually extend their schooling, obtaining vocational and technical qualifications.

People with stronger aptitudes are usually able to apply themselves to degree or professional courses. This group will, roughly, be the intellectual top 10 per cent and have an average IQ of 119.

The top 5 per cent have an IQ around 125. If you are very good at the tests, you may have an IQ which is around 135, which puts you into the top 1 per cent.

Remember to interpret your own score only as a general guide. If we assume that you might have a 'true' score this will not be revealed unless you are compared with people of the same age, sex and relevant background. It is best to assume that your own IQ from the table provided here is likely to be only a baseline estimate. Use it to ask yourself whether you are achieving what you would expect at college or in your career.

What tests should you use to calculate your IQ? It is possible to obtain an IQ on each one of the tests. The fairest estimate is probably to take the sum of several scores, then divide that number by the number of tests you have used.

Calculating 'overall IQ'

Test included: (up to 7)   'IQ' on test

_____   _____

_____   _____

_____   _____

_____   _____

_____   _____

_____   _____

_____   _____

Total of scores on tests = _____

Divide by (   ) number included = _____ 'Overall IQ'

Your IQ

	100	105	110	115	120	125	130	135	140	145
VERIFICATION	1–7	8–11	12–15	16–19	20–23	24–27	28–29	30–32	33–34	35–36
FORMATION	1–30	31–34	35–38	39–42	43–46	47–50	51–54	55–59	60–65	66–70
PHYSICAL ANALYSIS	1–5	6–8	9–10	11–12	13–15	16–17	18–20	21–23	24–26	27–28
VERBAL PENETRATION	1–11	12–16	17–20	21–24	25–28	29–32	33–36	37–38	39–40	41–42
NUMERICAL DEDUCTION	1–4	5–6	7	8–9	10–11	12–13	14–15	16–17	18–19	20–21
OBSERVATION	1–12	13–14	15–17	18–19	20–22	23–25	26–27	28–31	32–33	34–36
CRITICAL DISSECTION	1–9	10–11	12–13	14–15	16–17	18–20	21–24	25–28	29–31	32–33

Personality

Introduction

If Section 1 on motivation is about what you want to do, and Section 2 on aptitudes is about what you do best, then this section is about how you do it.

The reward for gaining knowledge about yourself is best experienced in applying it. Therefore this section provides you with a scheme for understanding your personality in such a way that you can direct yourself more effectively as a consequence. First, understanding your personality has relevance to career selection and, second, to the way in which you choose to gain the most from whatever you do and from the people you will have contact with at work.

Central to this section is a questionnaire which enables you to test the assumptions you have of yourself. Having obtained a measure of your personality, you can see how your own characteristics and style relate to different kinds of activity, and how your own contribution may complement those of others.

Personality

Although you behave in different ways, depending upon the circumstances you are in or the people you are with, you nevertheless have a personality that remains identifiable. If this were not true, people would not be able to anticipate your reactions; the very fact that there are aspects of you which are predictable testifies to your personality.

This is not to say that your personality will never change. It may well do so, especially if you make efforts to become aware of your potential and give yourself experiences which are developing. However, it seems practical to take your personality as it is now in order to see how it may relate more successfully to one career than another.

This book takes the premise that different careers do, by and large, require different characteristics. If you work at something which 'suits you' then you will avoid frustration, while your continuing satisfaction and enjoyment are more likely to be assured. It is also true that most careers can be done equally enjoyably by people with widely varying characteristics. It is bound to be so, since no two people are ever completely alike. However, in very broad terms, it makes sense to ask, 'In this career, how would my personality fit?' and, 'Would I enjoy and be successful in this career for the very reason that my personality might be unusual?'

At the end of this book, in the profile matching section, you will see how personality dimensions have been connected to careers. The way to use this is either to see which dimensions of your own fit with the careers, or to look at a career which appeals to you and see if your own dimensions match. If they don't, it does not suggest you would be unsuitable, but that you should think carefully about how your own personality could make you successful. It could be, of course, that although your personality does not seem to match exactly, your results from the aptitude or motivation sections do.

Personality is a complex subject. The aim here is to assist you to get to know yourself better and to ask you to consider what it is about the way you feel and behave that might make you more suited to one career than another. To do this, it is best to be honest as to how you see yourself. There are no rights or wrongs to a test of personality. What is wanted is a description of the real you. Now, just in case you 'undersell' or 'oversell' yourself, you could ask other people who are close to you and know you well to complete the questionnaire for the way they see you. If that means you have to photocopy the questionnaire, it is all right for you to do so for this purpose. Then compare your own responses with that of others.

The most accurate description of you is likely to be the person you are now, the way you behave and the person other people know and recognize. It is possible to answer the questionnaire on the basis of assuming how you think you want to be one day, but as you have not got there yet, you will need to think carefully what you have to do to change.

Another factor to consider is whether you might be using a part of your characteristics now, but want to use other parts later on as you develop in your career. For example, if you are factual you might enjoy studying for a scientific career, but later on, if you find yourself working at a laboratory bench, you may find it has too little opportunity for a gregarious personality.

Personality questionnaire

This questionnaire attempts to bring out some broad dimensions which are relevant to work. They can give you general guidance as to what is likely to provide you with continuing satisfaction and challenge.

Instructions

You are asked to think about a statement about yourself. If the statement describes you, put a tick through the Y ('Yes'). If the statement does not describe you, put a tick through the N ('No').

There are no 'right' or 'wrong' answers. The questionnaire is intended to gain a picture of your behaviour and the way you feel about life in general.

Answer each statement for the way you normally feel. All the statements must be completed to get a full picture of you.

As you complete the questionnaire try not to take any notice of the letters at the head of each column. These are to help you mark your results. How to do this will be explained when you have completed all the statements.

Part 1	So	G	A	P	I	F	Sp	D
1. I like to get on with my work without interference.	Y	N						
2. I go out of my way to make contact with new people.			Y	N				
3. I cannot feel relaxed unless I am certain I have made no mistakes.					Y	N		
4. I am frequently spontaneous in reacting to something that has happened.							Y	N
5. I have troubles which weigh me down.					Y	N		
6. The way I tackle a difficult problem is immediately.							N	Y
7. It is up to people if they keep their thoughts to themselves, I still say what I think.			Y	N				
8. I feel happier when supporting rather than taking the lead myself.			Y	N				
9. I like to stick with my group.	N	Y						
10. I try to protect people by not saying hurtful things.					Y	N		
11. I do not take on more than can be done thoroughly and properly.							N	Y
12. I tend to see the worst.					Y	N		
13. It often does not help to examine feelings too closely.					N	Y		
14. In the end, there's not much that bothers me.							N	Y
15. Teamwork gets the best from me.	N	Y						
16. I am a fairly quiet person.			N	Y				
17. Practical jokes amuse me.							Y	N
18. People do not always realize how hurtful their remarks can be.			N	Y				
19. I like to be with lots of witty, amusing people.							Y	N
20. I quickly get bored unless something exciting grabs my attention.							Y	N
21. I am cool under pressure.					N	Y		
22. I rarely get emotional.					N	Y		

	So	G	A	P	I	F	Sp	D
23. I do not like to be by myself for too long.	N	Y						
24. I am sometimes unsure about how well I fit in with other people.			N	Y				
25. I make sure that people hear what I have to say.			Y	N				
26. Instead of sleeping, I may get a bit anxious about things which could go wrong.					Y	N		
27. I share my thoughts and feelings.	N	Y						
28. I could not work long without having people around to mix with.	N	Y						
29. I prefer not to discuss with anyone what I am going to do.	Y	N						
30. I consider people disagreeing with me as a challenge.			Y	N				
31. I cannot bear having to concentrate on routine things.							Y	N
32. I like to be able to do things which have not been planned.							Y	N
33. People often look to me to take the lead.			Y	N				
34. I enjoy chatting about my life with a group of people I know.	N	Y						
35. I could not do anything that might hurt someone's feelings.					Y	N		
36. I am fairly quiet in a group.			N	Y				
37. I am prepared to shout loudly if it is necessary to make people understand.			Y	N				
38. I am happy with life and take it as it comes.							N	Y
39. I like people to ask before disturbing me.	Y	N						
40. It is more fun to be in a crowd than by myself.	N	Y						

In the second part, instead of answering how you see yourself, answer in the way you expect other people would describe you. Again, do not leave any statements unanswered.

Part 2	So	G	A	P	I	F	Sp	D
People would describe me as:								
1. Friendly.	N	Y						
2. Separate.	Y	N						
3. Even-tempered.							N	Y
4. Showy.			Y	N				
5. Reserved.			N	Y				
6. Easily upset.					Y	N		
7. A 'pushover'.	N	Y						
8. Fearless.			Y	N				
9. Hasty.							Y	N
10. Lively.							Y	N
11. Strong.			Y	N				
12. Go my own way.	Y	N						
13. Warm person.	N	Y						
14. Temperamental.					Y	N		
15. 'Like to be liked'.	N	Y						
16. Demonstrative.			Y	N				
17. Shy.			N	Y				
18. Welcoming.	N	Y						
19. Practical.					N	Y		
20. Spirited.							Y	N
21. Indifferent.					N	Y		
22. Meek.			N	Y				
23. Intuitive.							Y	N
24. Pliable.					Y	N		
25. Stunning.							Y	N
26. By oneself.	Y	N						
27. Passive.							N	Y
28. Plain-speaking.					N	Y		
29. 'Wrapped up' in myself.					Y	N		
30. Gentle.							N	Y
31. Solitary.	Y	N						
32. Precise.					N	Y		
33. Nervous.			N	Y				
34. Go-ahead.			Y	N				
35. Untroubled.							N	Y
36. Soft.					Y	N		
37. Restful.							N	Y
38. Unemotional.					N	Y		
39. Fearful.			N	Y				
40. On one's own.	Y	N						

Marking the questionnaire

To do this, you have to look at the number of times you have placed a tick in some of the columns under some of the letters.

In Part 1, count up the number of times you have placed a tick through either the 'Y' or the 'N' in the 'F' column. This is your F score, and can be placed in the chart for calculating your personality type, below.

Do the same thing with Part 2. The maximum score possible for each part is 10, so that adding your two scores together will give you a score out of 20.

Then do the same addition with the letters Sp, A and G.

If you wish, you can check you have done this correctly by adding the number of ticks you have made in column I. As letter I 'goes with' letter F, the total should be 20. This is the same for Sp with D, A with P, and G with So.

Chart for calculating personality dimensions

Part 1	+	Part 2	=	Total out of 20
F ....../10	+	F ....../10	=	........../20
Sp ....../10	+	Sp ....../10	=	........../20
A ....../10	+	A ....../10	=	........../20
G ....../10	+	G ....../10	=	........../20

Each of these scores relates to a broad dimension of personality relevant to your career. You can obtain a description of what these individual dimensions might mean. Then, it will be important what effect all of them might have when taken together.

Personality charts

Place your scores for Part 1 of the personality test in the first of the charts below. These are your results for how you perceive yourself.

Do the same thing with your scores for Part 2 of the test, putting these in the second of the charts below. These are your results for how you are perceived by others.

Finally, put your total score for both parts into the third of the charts below. These represent the complete measure of your personality.

Chart 1 – how you perceive yourself

Dimension	1 2 3 4 5	6 7 8 9 10	Dimension
I – Imaginative	– ╂ – – –	– – – – –	F – Factual
D – Deliberate	– – – – –	– – – ╂ –	Sp – Spontaneous
P – Passive	– – – ╂ –	– – – – –	A – Assertive
So – Solitary	╂– – – – –	– – – – –	G – Gregarious

Chart 2 – how you are perceived

Dimension	1 2 3 4 5	6 7 8 9 10	Dimension
I – Imaginative	– – – – –	– ╂ – – –	F – Factual
D – Deliberate	– – – – –	╂ – – – –	Sp – Spontaneous
P – Passive	– ✖ – – –	– – ╂ – –	A – Assertive
So – Solitary	– – – ╂ –	✖ – – – –	G – Gregarious

Chart 3 – your personality

Dimension	2 4 6 8 10	12 14 16 18 20	Dimension
I – Imaginative	– – – –╂–	– – – – –	F – Factual
D – Deliberate	– – – – –	– –╂– – –	Sp – Spontaneous
P – Passive	– – ✖ – –	╂– – – –	A – Assertive
So – Solitary	– ╂ ♠ – –	– – – – –	G – Gregarious

Understanding chart differences

The way you see yourself may be accurate, or not. To obtain some kind of accuracy check, you were asked to complete the second part of the questionnaire for the way others see you. Of course, you may imagine they see you in quite a different way from the way they actually do. The way they see you is best revealed if they are the ones who actually complete Part 2, without any interference from you. Then, we run into a further possible confusion: the way they see you may not be accurate either. In the end, who is to say whether the way you perceive yourself, or the way others perceive you is correct? This is why the combined totals from both parts are taken as the best overall picture of your personality. However, if there is a discrepancy between the two parts to the extent you think that the overall picture is inaccurate, then assume that the results of Part 1, chart 1, is your personality.

To develop your own awareness it could be a useful exercise to ask people why they see you in ways that are different from the way you see yourself. Perhaps you are underestimating your potential, thus missing some opportunities you should be considering. Perhaps you are unknowingly behaving in a manner which others put more importance upon than you do. The clearer you can be about your personality dimensions, the more assured you will be in finding the type of career which is best suited to you.

Dimensions and characteristics

Your 'characteristics' are formed from the eight letters which make up the opposite poles on the four dimensions. Thus, you are either So or G, A or P, I or F, Sp or D. The relevant letters can easily be read off from the position of your scores on chart 3 (or chart 1, if you prefer) above. These various combinations give 16 possible characteristics which are described below.

It may be that some of your scores were in the middle range (8 to 12). Your characteristics may not therefore emerge so clearly as those where the scores are distinctly at the low end or high end of each dimension. If this happens, you may need to look at a description of characteristics which is close. For example, if your characteristics are ISpPG, but your score on the G dimension was 12, you may find that you also have some behaviours or feelings that are very like the ISpPSo characteristics.

Write in the letters that summarize your characteristics:

_____

Interpretation

The personality questionnaire uses a logical scheme. First of all it divides behaviour into that which is task directed and that which is directed towards people. Task and people each has two components.

Within task the action is factual or imaginative; it is also impulsive or cautious.

Within people the objective is to determine whether behaviour is assertive or passive, group dependent or self-sufficient.

Clearly, your orientation towards the task and the manner in which you relate to people have implications for all careers.

The lower your score on each of the dimensions, the more you are like the descriptions on the left-hand side of the page. The higher your score on the dimension, the more you will be like the description on the right-hand side.

Not all of the words and descriptions will necessarily match you exactly. However, the general description they give is important in relation to different areas of work. If your scores are in the middle, your character on that description will not be extreme and you might at different times show some of the behaviours associated with both descriptions. The more your scores are at either end of the scale, the more likely it is that your approach and behaviour are consistent with the description.

0 1 2 3 4 5 6 7 8 9 10   11 12 13 14 15 16 17 18 19 20

I – IMAGINATIVE

Low scorers are more sensitive and aware of people's feelings. Emotional and often expressive. Make decisions with your heart rather than your head. Easily affected, hurt by criticism. Spend too much time on small things. Often discouraged and frustrated, but also intuitive and creative. Responsive to feelings and/or ideas.

D – DELIBERATE

Low scorers are calm, stable and dependable. They are patient in waiting for things to take their time. Composed and unflustered by events. Take things as they come. The slow, deliberate approach allows people to depend upon you. Could appear dull or unresponsive. Predictable. Smug – the type who says, 'I told you so'. Cope with pressure. Get things done in an orderly way.

P – PASSIVE

Low scorers are mild and tend not to push themselves onto others. They tend to keep matters to them-selves, giving way rather than arguing. Easy to get on with. Often good team members. Accommodating and not easily annoyed. May avoid saying what is on their mind. Avoid confrontation. Try hard to please. Cooperative, respectful and helpful.

F – FACTUAL

High scorers tend to be factual and see things logically. They tend to be composed and have their 'feet on the ground'. Like orderly, structured behaviour. Not easily distracted, do things in a controlled way. Objective and analytical, see the essential point. May miss subtle issues which bother others. Like information and facts.

Sp – SPONTANEOUS

High scorers are lively and impulsive. They like change and situations which are fast moving and different. Often they find it difficult to stick to one thing or to finish what they started. Amusing and enthusiastic, your excitement can infect others. You may be seen as lacking 'depth' as you chase from one thing to the next. Organization could be forgotten, though you might produce a great effect.

A – ASSERTIVE

High scorers are assertive, even aggressive. May be dominant and stubborn. Seen as 'pushy'. May talk loudly. Get the point across. Determined, sometimes risk-taking, get what they want. Can 'tread on toes'. May be seen as a 'show off' but also gain respect. May lose sight of how people are affected. Critical. Demanding. Take responsibility.

So – SOLITARY
Low-scorers feel they achieve best themselves. Self-reliant. Take initiative on their own. Show initiative. May be seen as either quiet or arrogant. 'Outsider' as an extreme. Work in own way. Can socialize but sometimes shy. Not at ease socially. Detached and purposeful. Make up own mind. Resourceful. Do not make 'small talk'.

G – GREGARIOUS
High scorers like lots of people around. Gregarious, fit in, not necessarily the leader. Seek company. Hate to be alone. Loyal and provide support. May be easily persuaded by the group out of need to be accepted. Change behaviour to fit in. Resolve differences between others. Participative, enjoy making decisions with others.

Dimensions and careers

I – IMAGINATIVE
artist, author (non-technical), dancer, florist, music therapist, musician, speech and drama teacher, window dresser

D – DELIBERATE
administrator, ambulance crew, draughts person, ergonomist, fireman, osteopath, restorer, security officer, surgeon, therapist, work study officer

P – PASSIVE
dietician, dressmaker, engraver, gamekeeper, gardener, patents examiner, potter, store keeper, technical author

So – SOLITARY
archaeologist, chiropodist, craftsperson, delivery person, farm worker, interpreter, photographer, programmer, silversmith, taxi driver, train driver, writer

F – FACTUAL
barrister, camera person, customs officer, diver, estate agent, mechanic, prison officer, technician, traffic warden

Sp – SPONTANEOUS
advertising assistant, bar person, dancer, demonstrator, dresser, hairdresser, masseur or masseuse, model, public relations assistant, retail assistant

A – ASSERTIVE
actor/actress, broker, club manager, courier, drama teacher, fashion buyer, hotel manager, negotiator, news editor, reporter, sales agent, transport manager

G – GREGARIOUS
airline cabin crew, auctioneer, club secretary, entertainment officer, house parent, play leader, publican, sailor, soldier, trainer, youth worker

Detailed personality analysis

In the chart below, you can see where your own characteristics are entered. It is a good idea to lightly shade in your own area with a pencil. This helps to locate your characteristics quickly when you return to the chart later. Since the chart covers the entire spectrum of personality, it is also a quick way to see how different are people you know from yourself.

Chart of personality characteristics

TASK	Factual	Factual	Imaginative	Imaginative	PEOPLE
Gregarious	FDAG	FSpAG	IDAG	ISpAG	Assertive
Gregarious	FDPG	FSpPG	IDPG	ISpPG	Passive
Solitary	FDASo	FSpASo �঺	IDASo	ISpASo	Assertive
Solitary	FDPSo	FSpPSo	IDPSo	ISpPSo ⊗	Passive
PEOPLE	Deliberate	Spontaneous	Deliberate	Spontaneous	TASK

In this chart, the two task dimensions, whether you are factual or imaginative, and whether you are spontaneous or deliberate, are arranged in the vertical columns. The two people dimensions, whether you are assertive or passive, and whether you are gregarious or solitary are arranged hoizontally. This produces a comprehensive scheme for all the possible combinations of behaviour and application.

Some broad deductions about you and your style can be made from the chart. First, it is possible to divide task and people into four areas to obtain the following:

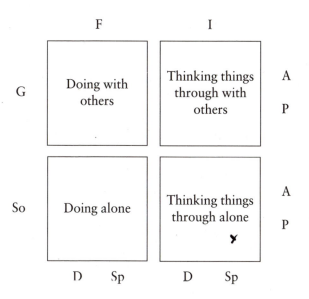

	F	I	
G	Doing with others	Thinking things through with others	A / P
So	Doing alone	Thinking things through alone ✗	A / P
	D Sp	D Sp	

Your typical relationship with people can be broadly determined by looking across the chart at the horizontal characteristics:

F or I

G	Commanders	A
G	Facilitators	P
So	Consultants	A
So	Supporters	P

D or Sp

Thus, if your characteristics are in the top horizontal line of the main chart, you will be a commander. In this case your style may vary from the factual and deliberate, to the imaginative and spontaneous.

Commanders

Assertive and gregarious, commanders like to take responsibility. They are influential and persuasive, often displaying energy and flair in directing others whatever the activity. Their enthusiasm often makes people turn to them for advice and leadership. As they have confidence and social skills, they usually rapidly assume a position at the head of any group.

There are four basic situations which will suit some commanders better than others. Some commanders flourish best in a situation where a measured, deliberate approach is best. Others are more suited to situations which require a more rapid, spontaneous approach. Others are suited to situations where ideas and possibilities have to be thoroughly processed in a deliberate manner. Others like to take ideas and act upon them immediately while the opportunity is present. However, often different commander styles mean that the same job is done just as well, but differently.

Facilitators

Passive and gregarious, facilitators use their acceptability within a group to draw out the best in people in any situation. They are frequently knowledgeable, but gain a good deal of respect by holding back as opposed to being pushy. They are likely to make others share responsibility for what happens. Their influence develops as they are seen as a resource and they are often viewed as a good monitor of what is happening.

Some facilitators may suit one situation better than others, depending upon their style. Some are most effective when working with others in a situation where facts have to be acquired and a careful, deliberate approach has to be worked out. Others will prefer a situation in which the facts can be used rapidly. Some are better at contributing in a more imaginative environment, while ensuring that ideas are processed carefully. Others like to work in a team where a rapid response to ideas and opportunities is required.

Consultants

Solitary and assertive, consultants seek to gain acceptance of their skills and knowledge. Often socially skilled, they nevertheless tend to work in their own way. They are often influential, drawing attention to matters on which they are expert. They rarely stay within a group for long, or they take up a peripheral position, coming into the centre of the group when they have something useful to add. Often, they become commanders on a temporary basis.

Consultants have four basic styles which suit them better in some situations than others. The first is one in which they show the way to deal with factual problems where a cautious and deliberate approach is required. Second, they may see ways of applying facts in a quick manner. Third, they may be best suited to dealing with new possibilities, while making sure that people do not get carried away by them. Finally, they may be best suited to situations where quick action is called for in order that opportunities can be taken advantage of while they last.

Supporters

Passive and solitary, supporters have the skills and resourcefulness to enable a project to succeed. As they do not include themselves, they generally have to be approached. They respond effectively when they are aware they are needed, but are reluctant to influence others unduly. They may prefer to add their contribution in their own way, rather than mix in or pool their efforts. They are often effective in assisting others to carry out a task.

Supporters may find themselves best suited to one of four situations. Some are suited to dealing with facts and analysis, approaching issues carefully and deliberately. Others like to be more spontaneous in taking an analytical approach, but acting rapidly. Others like to work with ideas, considering various possibilities in a planned deliberate way. Others like to act impulsively on the basis of ideas and opportunities which arise.

Your preferred, broad approach to the task can be determined by looking at the vertical characteristics:

	F	F	I	I	
G	Organizing	Implementing	Planning	Experimenting	A
G	Organizing	Implementing	Planning	Experimenting	P
S.	Organizing	Implementing	Planning	Experimenting	A
S.	Organizing	Implementing	Planning	Experimenting	P
	D	Sp	D	Sp	

Organizer

Factual and deliberate, organizers take an objective, systematic approach. Their virtue is that they are unlikely to be rushed, so that what they do can be relied upon. They are effective at dealing with information in a planned way, so that the best use may be gained from everything.

There are four basic types of organizer. Some are best suited to a situation in which they can take charge in a group of people. Others prefer a situation where people work together and responsibility for organization is shared. Others like to have their own area of responsibility and work largely by themselves, while taking charge when their own area of expertise is sought. Finally, some like to work in their own way and prefer it if others direct their efforts.

Implementer

Factual and spontaneous, implementers like to get things done. Having ascertained the facts, the application of knowledge or systems is what appeals to them. They are often best suited to undertaking tasks which need to be worked upon and completed in the short term, since they enjoy seeing the results of their efforts have an immediate effect.

Some implementers are best suited to managing people and other resources. Alternatively, they may prefer to have things carried out with the whole team so that they are not mainly responsible. Some implementers take responsibility for specific tasks, joining in with a group only when they have to. Finally, some implementers like to work in their own way and to be responsible for their own efforts.

Planner

Imaginative and deliberate, planners are careful to make sure that ideas are worked upon and shaped so that they will be most useful. A liking for work that is abstract yet has a practical application is typical of planners. Their contribution is that they can often see ways to do things, and they have the patience to see an idea through to fruition.

There are four basic styles for the planner. In the first, enjoyment is obtained by working in a group, persuading others as to the best plan and taking responsibility for developing it. In the second, a sharing of plans is preferred so that the end result is often a collective one. In the third, the preference is to work alone, but take charge on an occasional or project basis, when particular skills or knowledge are required. Finally, the preference is to work on plans alone.

Experimenter

Imaginative and spontaneous, experimenters like to use initiative and seek novelty. They are usually impatient with analysis and research, wanting excitement and immediate challenge. They are often courageous in having to live with failure, and often make things happen at the opportune time.

There are four basic situations for the experimenter. Some enjoy teams and taking responsibility for taking action. Others prefer a collaborative effort so that no experiment is a single person's responsibility. Some like to work by themselves, but will direct the efforts of others when they are affected by their own contribution or when it is necessary to get their own idea tested. Finally, others like to work entirely by themselves.

Team contribution

There are very few careers which do not have some interaction or contact with others. The amount and the nature of this 'interpersonal' part of your work are taken increasingly seriously in almost all organizations. This is because the manner in which people relate to each other can make or break the organization. It is therefore essential to have a career which gives you the balance you want between using skills and the appropriate kind of people contact. Not everybody has to be enthusiastic all the time about mixing socially. That is not what is meant. Teams also consist of people who do not need to mix very much, but whose contribution, when they are required to make it, is nevertheless vital for overall team performance.

An awareness of your typical style helps create awareness of the impact you are likely to have upon others, and may also help you to appreciate the contribution that others make, which is different simply because it is different from your own.

Chart of team styles

TASK	Factual	Factual	Imaginative	Imaginative	PEOPLE
Gregarious	Commanding Organizer	Commanding Implementer	Commanding Planner	Commanding Experimenter	Assertive
Gregarious	Facilitating Organizer	Facilitating Implementer	Facilitating Planner	Facilitating Experimenter	Passive
Solitary	Consulting Organizer	Consulting Implementer	Consulting Planner	Consulting Experimenter	Assertive
Solitary	Supporting Organizer	Supporting Implementer	Supporting Planner	Supporting Experimenter	Passive
PEOPLE	Deliberate	Spontaneous	Deliberate	Spontaneous	TASK

Description of personality titles

Remember that you are more clearly in one area than another if your scores are more at the extreme end of each dimension. Where your scores are around the middle range, you may consider that, on balance, an adjacent area might be more like you. For example, number 13, a researcher, might be number 9, an arranger, if a little more assertive.

Another point to bear in mind is that we are all capable of behaving in different ways on different occasions and in different circumstances. That is why, as members of teams, we often take on different roles and responsibilities, which might not be entirely suited to us but need to be done.

Chart of individual personality titles

TASK	Factual	Factual	Imaginative	Imaginative	PEOPLE
Gregarious	1. Director	2. Opportunist	3. Coach	4. Crusader	Assertive
Gregarious	5. Completer	6. Associate	7. Confidant	8. Colleague	Passive
Solitary	9. Arranger	10. Adviser	11. Designer	12. Idealist	Assertive
Solitary	13. Researcher	14. Implementer	15. Specialist	16. Wanderer	Passive
PEOPLE	Deliberate	Spontaneous	Deliberate	Spontaneous	TASK

1. FDAG – Director

Characteristics: Factual, Deliberate, Assertive and Gregarious.

Style: Commanding Organizer.

Description: energetic, resourceful, achiever, uses resources of people, makes things happen, plans ahead, uses personal flair, calm and controlled, responsible, experienced.

Possible points to improve: slowness to react, lack of imagination, overconfidence.

Careers: bank manager, general manager, hotel manager, officer in armed forces, production manager, retail manager, transport manager.

2. FSpAG – Opportunist

Characteristics: Factual, Spontaneous, Assertive and Gregarious.

Style: Commanding Implementer.

Description: persuasive, fast moving, energetic, often hard working, likes authority, shows flair, influential, an achiever.

Possible points to improve: lack of caution, taking on too many things, demanding, impatient.

Careers: advertising executive, auctioneer, club secretary, estate agent, funds organizer, politician, public relations director, senior administrator, sports coach or manager.

3. IDAG – Coach

Characteristics: Imaginative, Deliberate, Assertive and Gregarious.

Style: Commanding Planner.

Description: takes pressure, has authority, clear, purposeful, skilled with people, sensitive, caring, active, involved, firm, altruistic.

Possible points to improve: overprotective, too involved, identifies too strongly with others' problems.

Careers: doctor, osteopath, psychologist, senior nursing officer, senior teacher, social worker, youth worker.

4. ISpAG – Crusader

Characteristics: Imaginative, Spontaneous, Assertive and Gregarious.

Style: Commanding Experimenter.

Description: considerate, thoughtful, inspired, spontaneous, insightful, caring, active, idealistic, involved, intense.

Possible points to improve: impulsiveness, may 'tread on toes', too involved, demanding.

Careers: beautician, equal opportunities adviser, courier, demonstrator, drama teacher, journalist, public relations executive, union representative.

5. FDPG – Completer

Characteristics: Factual, Deliberate, Passive and Gregarious.

Style: Facilitating Organizer.

Description: 'people-person', adaptable, likeable, stable, reassuring, reasonable, orderly, practical, trustworthy.

Possible points to improve: conventional, predictable, unimaginative, easily led, accommodating.

Careers: ambulance crew, armed forces, cashier, fireman, guard, nurse, police officer, prison officer.

6. FSpPG – Associate

Characteristics: Factual, Spontaneous, Passive and Gregarious.

Style: Facilitating Implementer.

Description: stable, dependable, conforms, exceptional team member, resourceful, tactful, understanding, reassuring, popular, enthusiastic, capable.

Possible points to improve: tends to give way, avoids conflict, taken advantage of, underuses potential.

Careers: airline cabin crew, bar person, dental assistant, hairdresser, junior teacher, play leader, secretary, sports or gym assistant, team leader.

7. IDPG – Confidant

Characteristics: Imaginative, Deliberate, Passive and Gregarious.

Style: Facilitating Planner.

Description: insightful, skilled, thoughtful, sympathetic, tactful, discreet, caring, democratic, resourceful.

Possible points to improve: indulgence, compliance.

Careers: hospital porter, house parent, mental nurse, nursery teacher, remedial teacher, social worker, therapist.

8. ISpPG – Colleague

Characteristics: Imaginative, Spontaneous, Passive and Gregarious.

Style: Facilitating Experimenter.

Description: responsive, experimenting, curious, eager, impulsive, team person, friendly, empathetic, enthusiastic, fun.

Possible points to improve: easily bored, not a finisher, lacks caution, disorganized, unsettled.

Careers: counsellor, marketing assistant, nursery nurse, receptionist, retail assistant, stagehand, waiter/waitress.

9. FDASo – Arranger

Characteristics: Factual, Deliberate, Assertive and Solitary.

Style: Consulting Organizer.

Description: factual, analytical, formidable, clear, cool, sharp, penetrating, self-reliant, business-like, detached, assertive, clever.

Possible points to improve: unsentimental, competitive, sceptical, detached, intolerant.

Careers: barrister, customs officer, police inspector, solicitor, tax inspector, work study officer.

10. FSpASo – Adviser

Characteristics: Factual, Spontaneous, Assertive and Solitary.

Style: Consulting Implementer.

Description: determined, single-minded, purposeful, energetic, sees opportunities, persistent, enterprising, takes initiative, impatient.

Possible points to improve: does not consider feelings, exploits others, appears selfish, aggressive.

Careers: buyer, club manager, commodities or futures broker, entrepreneur, importer/exporter, market trader, property speculator, road manager, sales director.

11. IDASo – Designer

Characteristics: Imaginative, Deliberate, Assertive and Solitary.

Style: Consulting Planner.

Description: objective, educated, thoughtful, influential, consultant, shows initiative, conceptual, persuasive, steady.

Possible points to improve: critical, outsider, remote, theoretical, too abstract, dogmatic, uncompromising.

Careers: analyst, architect, business consultant, journalist, librarian, medical scientist, social scientist.

12. ISpASo – Idealist

Characteristics: Imaginative, Spontaneous, Assertive and Solitary.

Style: Consulting Experimenter.

Description: expressive, imaginative, inquisitive, reflective, emotional, challenging, complex, perceptive.

Possible points to improve: impractical, easily hurt, sceptical, defensive, intolerant, emotional.

Careers: architect, artist, author, dancer, interior designer, musician, sculptor.

13. FDPSo – Researcher

Characteristics: Factual, Deliberate, Passive and Solitary.

Style: Supporting Organizer.

Description: detached, objective, problem-solver, informed, curious, technical, straightforward, efficient, orderly, knowledgeable.

Possible points to improve: serious, brusque, dismissive, aloof, cool, intolerant.

Careers: accounting technician, actuary, archivist, auditor, driver, engineer, operations researcher, reinsurer.

14. FSpPSo – Implementer

Characteristics: Factual, Spontaneous, Passive and Solitary.

Style: Supporting Implementer.

Description: self-reliant, lively, capable in own work, adaptable, fits in easily while detached, takes responsibility for self – does not want authority, reliable, detached, skilled.

Possible points to improve: not a risk-taker, passive, not effective when working through others, impulsive.

Careers: accounting technician, chef, IT technician, dietician, interpreter, paramedic, road patrol officer, surgeon, tour guide.

15. IDPSo – Specialist

Characteristics: Imaginative, Deliberate, Passive and Solitary.

Style: Supporting Planner.

Description: solitary, intelligent, thoughtful, inquiring, aware, creative, insightful, loyal, sincere, sensitive, straightforward, direct.

Possible points to improve: unadventurous, blunt, awkward, embarrassed, unassuming.

Careers: arborist, curator, delivery person, farm worker, gardener, gun-maker, historian, planner, potter, saddler, shepherd, site worker, thatcher.

16. ISpPSo – Wanderer

Characteristics: Imaginative, Spontaneous, Passive and Solitary.

Style: Supporting Experimenter.

Description: 'jack of all trades', knowledgable, entertaining, quick-witted, self-reliant, imaginative, inquisitive.

Possible points to improve: restless, unreliable, disorganized, neglectful, impetuous, procrastinates.

Careers: bar person, dancer, disc jockey, entertainer, model, porter, production worker, shop assistant, waiter/waitress.

4

Profile matching

There are two ways of using the Profile Section.

- Looking down the list of careers and checking out what character-istics are required, seeing if yours match.
- Looking down the pattern of characteristics, stopping at those occu-pations which seem closely to match your own.

Considerable caution, as well as intuition, are required to obtain the most from matching your own characteristics to the profiles which follow. The issues regarding this exercise have largely been discussed already in the Introduction. Some guidelines are provided here:

- in the following pages of occupations, ticks are placed to give an indi-cation of the most likely characteristics associated with that occu-pation. These are not the only possible ones. Where you do not have the characteristics suggested, but like the sound of the occupation, always ask yourself how your own characteristics might also be suitable;
- where your characteristics in one area, say motivation, coincide with many possible occupations, use the aptitudes and personality areas to narrow down the possibilities;
- ticks in the aptitudes area indicate where some potential is likely to be required. In relation to occupations which might require a degree as a starting point, potential is likely to be required at least at the level of 'good evidence'.

Code

Motivation

W	Words
A	Art
P	Practical
E	Experimenting
O	Organizing
B	Business
S	Social

Aptitudes

Ve	Verification
F	Formation
P	Physical Reasoning
V	Verbal Penetration
N	Numerical Deduction
O	Observation
C	Critical Dissection

Personality

F	Factual
I	Imaginative
Sp	Spontaneous
D	Deliberate
A	Assertive
P	Passive
G	Gregarious
So	Solitary

	W	A	P	E	O	B	S	Ve	F	P	V	N	O	C	F	I	Sp	D	A	P	G	So
Accident Assessor			✓		✓			✓	✓		✓			✓			✓					
Accountant					✓	✓					✓	✓		✓			✓	✓				
Accounting Technician				✓							✓			✓			✓		✓			
Actor	✓	✓									✓					✓	✓					
Actuary			✓	✓			✓				✓	✓	✓	✓			✓					
Acupuncturist		✓	✓			✓		✓					✓				✓		✓			
Administrator	✓			✓							✓	✓		✓			✓					
Advertising Copywriter	✓										✓					✓						
Advertising Executive		✓				✓					✓	✓								✓		✓
Advertising Space Sales Person					✓											✓	✓	✓	✓			✓
Aerobics Instructor		✓	✓			✓		✓				✓					✓		✓		✓	
Aeronautical Engineer			✓	✓				✓	✓		✓			✓			✓					
Aeronautical Technician			✓	✓				✓	✓					✓			✓	✓				
Agricultural Mechanic			✓				✓							✓			✓	✓				✓
Agricultural Secretary	✓		✓					✓									✓					
Agriculturalist			✓	✓							✓	✓		✓			✓					
Air Traffic Controller			✓	✓			✓	✓			✓			✓			✓	✓				✓
Ambulance Crew			✓			✓								✓			✓	✓				

	W	A	P	E	O	B	S	Ve	F	P	V	N	O	C	F	I	Sp	D	A	P	G	So
Anaesthetist				✓		✓					✓	✓		✓			✓		✓			✓
Animal Keeper			✓																✓			✓
Animal Nurse			✓											✓					✓			✓
Anthropologist	✓	✓		✓					✓		✓	✓										✓
Antique Dealer		✓				✓			✓									✓				
Arborist		✓	✓						✓										✓			✓
Architect		✓							✓		✓	✓		✓				✓	✓			✓
Architectural Technician		✓							✓					✓				✓	✓			✓
Archivist	✓			✓							✓			✓				✓	✓			✓
Armed Forces Officer			✓			✓	✓		✓	✓				✓				✓			✓	
Armed Forces Personnel			✓			✓								✓							✓	
Aromatherapist		✓				✓								✓	✓				✓	✓		
Art Dealer		✓				✓			✓					✓				✓				
Art Restorer		✓	✓						✓					✓								✓
Art Therapist		✓				✓			✓	✓				✓					✓			✓
Artist		✓							✓					✓								✓
Arts Administrator	✓	✓		✓			✓				✓	✓		✓							✓	
Astronaut			✓	✓					✓	✓	✓	✓	✓	✓		✓			✓			
Astronomer				✓							✓	✓		✓		✓			✓			✓
Auctioneer						✓								✓		✓		✓				✓
Audiology Technician				✓				✓						✓	✓				✓			✓
Auditor				✓		✓					✓			✓	✓			✓	✓			✓
Author	✓								✓					✓		✓						✓
Automobile Technician			✓						✓	✓				✓					✓			✓
Bacteriologist				✓							✓	✓		✓					✓			✓
Baggage Handler			✓																			✓
Baker		✓					✓									✓			✓			✓
Ballet Dancer		✓													✓	✓			✓			
Bank Clerk				✓			✓		✓					✓				✓	✓			
Bank Manager				✓	✓		✓					✓		✓				✓	✓		✓	
Bar Person			✓												✓	✓			✓	✓		
Barrister	✓					✓					✓	✓		✓	✓				✓			
Beautician		✓					✓		✓						✓	✓				✓		
Bicycle Repairer			✓					✓											✓			✓
Bilingual Secretary	✓								✓					✓					✓			✓
Biologist				✓							✓	✓		✓					✓			✓
Biomedical Engineer			✓	✓				✓			✓			✓				✓	✓			✓
Boat Builder		✓	✓						✓	✓									✓			✓
Book Binder		✓							✓										✓			✓
Book Critic	✓					✓					✓			✓	✓	✓						✓
Book Illustrator		✓							✓					✓					✓			✓
Bookseller						✓												✓				
Botanist				✓								✓						✓	✓			✓

	W	A	P	E	O	B	S	Ve	F	P	V	N	O	C	F	I	Sp	D	A	P	G	So
Brewer			✓	✓											✓							
Bricklayer		✓							✓									✓	✓			✓
Broker					✓						✓			✓			✓		✓			
Builder's Merchant					✓						✓			✓								
Building Demolition Expert			✓						✓									✓	✓			✓
Building Inspector			✓	✓					✓					✓				✓	✓			✓
Building Society Assistant			✓					✓						✓				✓	✓			
Building Society Manager		✓	✓	✓				✓			✓			✓				✓			✓	
Building Surveyor				✓					✓		✓			✓				✓	✓			✓
Bursar			✓					✓			✓			✓				✓	✓			
Bus Driver		✓																	✓			✓
Business Consultant					✓						✓	✓	✓			✓						
Buyer	✓				✓				✓		✓					✓		✓	✓			
Cabin Crew	✓	✓				✓										✓	✓		✓	✓	✓	
Cabinet Maker	✓							✓								✓		✓	✓			✓
Camera Repairer			✓					✓	✓							✓			✓			✓
Car Body Designer	✓								✓							✓	✓		✓			
Careers Adviser					✓						✓			✓					✓			
Carpenter	✓								✓							✓			✓			✓
Cartographer	✓								✓									✓	✓			✓
Cartoon Animator	✓								✓							✓		✓	✓			✓
Cashier				✓			✓				✓			✓				✓	✓			
Caterer	✓			✓					✓								✓		✓		✓	
CD ROM Producer	✓					✓			✓		✓					✓	✓		✓			
Chef	✓								✓							✓	✓		✓			✓
Chemical Technician				✓								✓		✓		✓			✓			✓
Chemical Technologist				✓							✓	✓		✓		✓			✓			✓
Chemist				✓							✓	✓	✓	✓		✓						✓
Chief Executive				✓							✓	✓						✓				
Childcare Worker						✓														✓	✓	
Chiropodist			✓			✓						✓				✓			✓			✓
Choreographer		✓														✓	✓					
Cinema Manager		✓				✓										✓		✓	✓		✓	
Civil Engineer			✓	✓					✓		✓			✓		✓						
Civil Servant				✓			✓				✓	✓		✓		✓						
Clerk			✓								✓			✓		✓			✓			
Clinical Psychologist			✓			✓					✓	✓	✓	✓					✓			
Clown	✓															✓	✓		✓			
Club Manager					✓											✓			✓		✓	
Coastguard		✓																✓	✓			
College Admissions Counsellor				✓		✓								✓					✓			
Comic Illustrator		✓							✓							✓			✓			✓
Commercial Account Manager				✓	✓									✓					✓			

	W	A	P	E	O	B	S	Ve	F	P	V	N	O	C	F	I	Sp	D	A	P	G	So
Community Social Worker							✓									✓			✓	✓		
Community Warden							✓									✓			✓	✓		
Company Secretary	✓			✓			✓		✓	✓				✓				✓		✓		✓
Compositor		✓														✓		✓		✓		✓
Computer Animator		✓		✓				✓								✓		✓				
Computer Game Designer		✓					✓	✓			✓	✓				✓	✓			✓		✓
Computer Hardware Designer			✓	✓				✓	✓		✓			✓				✓				
Computer Systems Analyst			✓	✓			✓				✓	✓	✓					✓				✓
Confectioner		✓						✓								✓				✓		
Conference Organizer		✓		✓														✓	✓		✓	
Conservation Officer		✓		✓														✓	✓	✓		✓
Copywriter	✓										✓			✓		✓						✓
Coroner	✓			✓							✓	✓	✓	✓				✓	✓			
Cost Accountant				✓			✓				✓			✓				✓	✓			
Counsellor						✓										✓	✓		✓	✓		
Courier		✓																✓				✓
Court Reporter	✓										✓			✓				✓				✓
Crane Operator			✓																			✓
Criminologist	✓										✓	✓	✓					✓	✓			
Cruise Director						✓												✓			✓	
Cryptographer	✓						✓				✓	✓	✓	✓	✓			✓		✓		✓
Cultural Anthropologist	✓	✓		✓							✓	✓	✓				✓		✓			✓
Curator	✓	✓									✓	✓				✓		✓	✓			✓
Currency Trader						✓					✓			✓				✓	✓		✓	
Customer Services Manager				✓		✓												✓	✓	✓		
Customs Officer			✓	✓										✓				✓	✓			✓
Dance Instructor		✓				✓										✓	✓				✓	
Dancer		✓														✓	✓					
Deaf Interpreter						✓													✓			
Decorator		✓														✓						✓
Demonstrator					✓													✓	✓			
Dental Assistant				✓		✓						✓		✓				✓	✓			
Dental Hygienist				✓		✓						✓		✓				✓	✓			
Dental Nurse				✓		✓						✓		✓				✓	✓			
Dental Technician			✓	✓					✓	✓		✓		✓				✓	✓			✓
Dentist				✓		✓		✓			✓	✓		✓				✓	✓			
Dermatologist				✓							✓	✓		✓				✓	✓			✓
Design Engineer		✓					✓	✓			✓					✓		✓				
Designer		✓						✓								✓	✓					✓
Dietician				✓								✓		✓					✓			✓
Director (Media)	✓	✓				✓					✓			✓		✓			✓		✓	
Disc Jockey		✓														✓	✓	✓		✓		
Dispensing Optician				✓		✓					✓	✓		✓				✓	✓			✓

	W	A	P	E	O	B	S	Ve	F	P	V	N	O	C	F	I	Sp	D	A	P	G	So
Display Artist		✓						✓								✓	✓		✓			
Diver		✓						✓	✓					✓				✓	✓			✓
Doctor of Medicine				✓			✓				✓	✓	✓	✓				✓	✓			
Drama Teacher	✓						✓			✓				✓		✓	✓		✓		✓	
Draughtsperson		✓				✓	✓											✓	✓			✓
Dresser (Stage)		✓						✓								✓	✓	✓	✓			✓
Dressmaker		✓	✓					✓								✓	✓	✓	✓			✓
Driver		✓																✓	✓			✓
Drug and Alcohol Counsellor						✓										✓			✓			
Dry-cleaner					✓									✓					✓			
Ecologist				✓							✓					✓		✓	✓			
Economist				✓						✓		✓	✓			✓						
Editor	✓						✓		✓					✓		✓		✓	✓			
Editor (Newspaper)	✓				✓		✓		✓					✓		✓	✓	✓			✓	
Editorial Cartoonist		✓					✓							✓		✓	✓	✓				
Educational Psychologist				✓		✓			✓	✓	✓							✓				✓
Electrical Engineer			✓	✓		✓	✓				✓			✓				✓				
Electrician		✓												✓				✓				✓
Electronics Engineer			✓	✓		✓	✓				✓			✓				✓				✓
Embalmer		✓					✓											✓	✓			✓
Employment Officer				✓		✓												✓				
Engineering Pattern Manager			✓	✓			✓							✓				✓	✓			✓
Engineering Technician		✓										✓		✓				✓				
English Language Teacher	✓						✓		✓					✓		✓	✓	✓				
Engraver		✓					✓									✓	✓	✓				✓
Entertainments Officer		✓		✓												✓	✓					
Environmental Health Officer			✓	✓								✓		✓				✓				✓
Equestrian		✓																	✓			
Ergonomist			✓	✓		✓	✓					✓		✓				✓	✓			✓
Estate Agent				✓	✓													✓			✓	
Estate Manager			✓	✓	✓													✓	✓			
Exhibition Organizer		✓		✓												✓	✓	✓			✓	
Explosives Expert			✓	✓			✓	✓	✓			✓		✓				✓				✓
Farm Manager		✓		✓										✓				✓	✓			
Farm Worker		✓																	✓			✓
Farmer		✓			✓														✓			✓
Fashion Buyer		✓			✓			✓								✓	✓		✓			
Fashion Designer		✓						✓								✓	✓			✓		
Film Projectionist		✓												✓						✓		✓
Film Reviewer	✓	✓									✓			✓								✓
Financial Analyst				✓							✓			✓				✓	✓			✓
Financial Controller				✓	✓		✓				✓			✓				✓	✓			

	W	A	P	E	O	B	S	Ve	F	P	V	N	O	C	F	I	Sp	D	A	P	G	So
Fireman			✓														✓					✓
Fisheries Officer			✓											✓			✓					
Fisherman			✓																			✓
Fitter			✓						✓	✓								✓				✓
Flight Attendant						✓									✓		✓	✓	✓			
Florist		✓													✓	✓		✓				✓
Flyman (Theatre)			✓												✓	✓		✓				✓
Food Hygiene Inspector				✓								✓		✓				✓	✓			
Food Service Worker			✓																	✓		
Foreign Correspondent	✓										✓			✓	✓	✓		✓				✓
Foreign Language Teacher	✓					✓					✓				✓	✓		✓				
Forensic Pathologist			✓				✓				✓	✓		✓				✓	✓			✓
Forensic Psychologist			✓				✓		✓	✓	✓	✓	✓	✓				✓	✓			✓
Forensic Scientist			✓				✓				✓	✓		✓				✓	✓			✓
Forester				✓														✓				✓
Freelance Writer	✓										✓			✓	✓	✓		✓				✓
Fund Raiser					✓	✓									✓			✓	✓		✓	✓
Funeral Director				✓		✓								✓				✓	✓			
Furniture Maker		✓	✓						✓						✓			✓		✓		✓
Gamekeeper			✓															✓				
Gardener		✓	✓															✓				✓
Genealogist			✓				✓						✓	✓				✓	✓			✓
Geneticist			✓								✓	✓		✓				✓				✓
Geochemist			✓				✓				✓	✓		✓				✓	✓			✓
Geologist			✓				✓				✓	✓		✓				✓	✓			✓
Glass-blower		✓					✓											✓				✓
Glazier		✓	✓				✓											✓				
Golf Professional			✓		✓														✓		✓	
Graphic Designer		✓					✓								✓	✓		✓				✓
Grocer					✓													✓	✓			
Groundsman			✓															✓	✓			✓
Guard			✓											✓				✓				✓
Gunsmith		✓	✓				✓											✓	✓			✓
Hairdresser		✓					✓	✓							✓	✓				✓		
Head Teacher				✓			✓		✓	✓	✓			✓				✓		✓		
Health Services Administrator				✓				✓						✓				✓				
Health Visitor							✓					✓		✓				✓	✓			
Heating Engineer			✓						✓					✓								✓
Historian	✓		✓						✓		✓		✓					✓				✓
Homeopath			✓									✓		✓				✓	✓			
Horologist			✓					✓										✓	✓			✓
Horticulturalist		✓	✓				✓				✓							✓				✓

	W	A	P	E	O	B	S	Ve	F	P	V	N	O	C	F	I	Sp	D	A	P	G	So
Hospital Physicist			✓						✓		✓	✓		✓			✓		✓			
Hospital Porter			✓																✓			
Hostel Warden						✓															✓	
Hotel Manager					✓	✓												✓			✓	
House Parent						✓													✓		✓	
Housing Manager			✓			✓		✓						✓			✓		✓			
Human Resources Manager				✓	✓	✓					✓							✓				
Hydrographic Surveyor			✓						✓			✓		✓			✓					✓
Hydrologist			✓						✓		✓			✓			✓		✓		✓	✓
Illustrator		✓							✓							✓	✓					✓
Immunologist			✓								✓	✓		✓			✓		✓			
Importer/exporter				✓	✓						✓							✓				
Industrial Designer		✓					✓	✓								✓	✓					
Industrial Nurse			✓			✓						✓		✓			✓		✓			
Industrial Relations Officer				✓	✓													✓				
Information Officer	✓										✓					✓		✓		✓		
Information Scientist	✓		✓								✓	✓		✓			✓		✓		✓	✓
Instrument and Control Engineer			✓	✓				✓	✓		✓			✓			✓		✓		✓	✓
Instrument Maker			✓	✓			✓	✓	✓					✓			✓		✓			
Insurance Adjuster						✓			✓			✓		✓			✓					
Insurance Agent						✓			✓			✓		✓			✓	✓				✓
Interior Designer		✓						✓								✓	✓					
Interpreter	✓									✓						✓	✓			✓		✓
Interviewer	✓						✓									✓			✓			
IT Technician			✓	✓				✓	✓	✓		✓			✓		✓		✓		✓	
Jewellery Maker		✓							✓							✓	✓			✓		✓
Jockey		✓															✓	✓				
Joiner		✓	✓						✓										✓			✓
Journalist	✓							✓			✓					✓	✓		✓			
Judge	✓									✓			✓				✓	✓				✓
Justices Clerk	✓	✓			✓			✓									✓					✓
Laboratory Technician				✓								✓		✓			✓		✓			
Landscape Architect		✓					✓	✓			✓					✓	✓					✓
Language Teacher	✓					✓				✓						✓	✓		✓			
Lawyer	✓							✓			✓		✓				✓	✓				
Legal Executive	✓							✓			✓						✓		✓			
Leisure Centre Staff		✓	✓		✓			✓	✓								✓				✓	
Librarian	✓			✓	✓			✓			✓		✓			✓		✓	✓			✓
Library Assistant	✓				✓			✓								✓		✓	✓			✓
Lighting Technician		✓	✓						✓						✓		✓		✓			✓
Linguist	✓							✓			✓					✓	✓			✓	✓	

	W	A	P	E	O	B	S	Ve	F	P	V	N	O	C	F	I	Sp	D	A	P	G	So
Literary Agent	✓					✓				✓						✓	✓	✓				
Literary Critic	✓									✓				✓		✓	✓		✓			
Locksmith			✓				✓							✓		✓						✓
Lorry Driver			✓																	✓		✓
Machinist	✓	✓																		✓		✓
Maintenance Technician		✓						✓						✓				✓		✓		
Maitre D'		✓														✓	✓		✓		✓	
Make-up Artist		✓					✓									✓	✓					
Management Consultant				✓					✓	✓				✓		✓			✓		✓	
Managing Director				✓					✓	✓						✓	✓		✓			
Marine Biologist			✓						✓	✓				✓		✓			✓			
Market Gardener	✓	✓				✓										✓	✓					
Market Researcher			✓	✓			✓									✓	✓	✓				
Marketing Manager		✓				✓					✓					✓	✓	✓				
Masseur/Masseuse		✓					✓		✓							✓	✓			✓		
Materials Scientist			✓						✓	✓	✓	✓		✓		✓						
Mathematician			✓								✓			✓			✓					
Mechanic		✓					✓							✓		✓			✓			✓
Mechanical Engineer		✓	✓				✓		✓					✓		✓						
Medical Illustrator		✓	✓				✓							✓		✓	✓		✓			✓
Medical Records Officer				✓			✓							✓		✓						
Medical Representative			✓	✓													✓	✓				✓
Medical Secretary				✓			✓	✓								✓	✓		✓			
Mental Health Nurse			✓				✓					✓				✓	✓			✓	✓	
Merchandiser	✓		✓				✓									✓	✓		✓			
Merchant Seaman		✓												✓		✓			✓			✓
Metallurgist			✓				✓				✓	✓		✓		✓						
Meteorologist			✓				✓					✓		✓		✓			✓			✓
Microbiologist			✓									✓		✓		✓						✓
Midwife			✓			✓								✓		✓	✓		✓			
Milkman		✓															✓		✓			✓
Miller	✓	✓														✓						
Milliner	✓						✓									✓	✓		✓			✓
Miner		✓															✓		✓	✓	✓	
Minister of Religion						✓										✓		✓				✓
Model (Fashion)	✓															✓	✓					
Model Maker	✓	✓					✓	✓	✓							✓		✓	✓			✓
Museum Assistant	✓		✓													✓		✓	✓			
Music Producer	✓			✓										✓			✓		✓			
Music Therapist	✓					✓										✓	✓		✓			
Musician	✓															✓	✓		✓			

	W	A	P	E	O	B	S	Ve	F	P	V	N	O	C	F	I	Sp	D	A	P	G	So
Nanny						✓										✓	✓		✓			
Nature Conservancy Warden			✓	✓												✓		✓				✓
Navigating Officer			✓	✓				✓	✓		✓				✓			✓		✓		
Negotiator				✓											✓		✓		✓			
Neurosurgeon			✓					✓	✓		✓	✓			✓			✓				
Notary Public	✓						✓				✓			✓				✓		✓		
Novelist	✓										✓					✓	✓					✓
Nuclear Physicist			✓				✓				✓	✓			✓			✓				
Nurse			✓									✓			✓			✓		✓	✓	
Nursery Nurse			✓													✓	✓		✓			
Nutritionist			✓				✓					✓			✓			✓		✓		✓
Obstetrician			✓				✓		✓	✓		✓	✓		✓			✓				
Occupational Psychologist			✓		✓	✓				✓	✓	✓	✓	✓	✓			✓	✓			
Occupational Therapist		✓	✓				✓		✓							✓		✓		✓		✓
Office Cleaner			✓															✓		✓		✓
Office Manager				✓	✓		✓				✓				✓			✓	✓			
Oil Rig Worker			✓						✓						✓		✓			✓		
Operational Researcher			✓				✓				✓	✓	✓	✓				✓				✓
Opthalmic Optician			✓				✓					✓			✓			✓		✓		
Optician (Dispensing)			✓		✓		✓				✓	✓			✓		✓		✓			
Organization and Methods Officer			✓	✓			✓	✓		✓	✓				✓			✓				
Orthodontist			✓			✓		✓				✓			✓			✓		✓		
Orthoptist			✓					✓				✓			✓			✓		✓		
Osteopath		✓	✓				✓		✓						✓			✓	✓			✓
Outplacement Consultant				✓	✓										✓			✓	✓		✓	
Panel Beater			✓					✓										✓				✓
Paramedic			✓			✓									✓			✓				
Patent Agent	✓				✓		✓			✓			✓	✓				✓	✓			
Patent Examiner	✓		✓				✓			✓		✓	✓	✓				✓		✓		✓
Pathologist			✓				✓				✓	✓	✓	✓				✓				
Pattern Cutter		✓	✓				✓								✓			✓		✓		
Personal Trainer						✓											✓		✓		✓	
Pharmacist			✓		✓						✓	✓			✓			✓	✓			
Pharmacologist			✓								✓	✓			✓			✓		✓		✓
Philosopher	✓								✓				✓			✓	✓					✓
Photographer		✓					✓									✓	✓		✓			✓
Photographic Technician		✓	✓				✓	✓							✓			✓		✓		✓
Physicist			✓								✓	✓			✓			✓		✓		✓
Physiotherapist		✓		✓			✓		✓		✓		✓			✓	✓			✓		✓
Piano Teacher		✓					✓									✓	✓		✓			
Piano Tuner		✓							✓							✓	✓					✓
Picture Framer		✓					✓									✓	✓					✓

	W	A	P	E	O	B	S	Ve	F	P	V	N	O	C	F	I	Sp	D	A	P	G	So
Pilot (Airplane)			✓	✓				✓			✓	✓			✓		✓		✓	✓		✓
Pilot (Coastal)			✓					✓							✓		✓					
Plasterer		✓	✓					✓						✓	✓							✓
Play Leader						✓								✓	✓				✓	✓	✓	
Plumber			✓						✓						✓							✓
Poet	✓										✓					✓	✓		✓			✓
Police Dog Handler			✓												✓							✓
Police Officer			✓			✓												✓	✓			
Political Agent	✓					✓					✓			✓					✓		✓	
Politician						✓	✓										✓		✓	✓		
Pool and Spa Operator			✓											✓								
Post Office Clerk				✓							✓							✓	✓			
Poster Designer		✓					✓	✓								✓	✓		✓			✓
Postman/woman			✓															✓	✓			✓
Potter		✓						✓								✓	✓		✓			✓
Press Agent	✓										✓					✓	✓		✓		✓	
Primary School Teacher						✓											✓		✓			
Principal Nursing Officer				✓		✓					✓	✓	✓	✓				✓	✓		✓	
Printer		✓	✓				✓	✓								✓			✓	✓		✓
Prison Officer			✓			✓								✓					✓	✓		
Probation Officer						✓													✓	✓		
Producer (Films)		✓			✓	✓		✓			✓	✓				✓			✓	✓	✓	
Production Manager		✓	✓				✓									✓	✓		✓		✓	
Programmer				✓	✓		✓	✓			✓	✓			✓				✓	✓		✓
Property Negotiator						✓									✓			✓	✓			
Prosthetics Engineer			✓	✓			✓	✓							✓				✓	✓		✓
Psychiatric Social Worker						✓					✓			✓		✓	✓		✓			✓
Psychiatrist	✓		✓			✓					✓		✓			✓		✓	✓			✓
Psychoanalyst	✓					✓					✓			✓		✓	✓		✓			✓
Psychologist				✓		✓					✓	✓	✓						✓			✓
Psychotherapist	✓	✓				✓					✓	✓				✓	✓		✓			✓
Public Relations Executive	✓	✓				✓					✓					✓		✓	✓	✓	✓	
Publican			✓											✓				✓	✓		✓	
Publicity Agent	✓	✓				✓					✓					✓	✓		✓		✓	
Publisher	✓					✓					✓	✓				✓		✓	✓			
Purchasing Manager				✓	✓		✓				✓			✓				✓	✓			
Purser				✓			✓				✓			✓				✓	✓			
Quality Controller			✓	✓			✓		✓					✓	✓		✓					
Quality Inspector			✓				✓		✓					✓	✓			✓	✓			✓
Quantity Surveyor			✓	✓			✓	✓			✓				✓		✓		✓			✓
Racing Car Driver		✓													✓		✓		✓			
Radiographer				✓								✓			✓		✓		✓			✓

	W	A	P	E	O	B	S	Ve	F	P	V	N	O	C	F	I	Sp	D	A	P	G	So
Rating Valuation Officer				✓			✓				✓				✓		✓					
Receptionist	✓	✓					✓									✓	✓			✓	✓	✓
Recording Engineer			✓									✓			✓		✓			✓		✓
Reflexologist		✓		✓			✓									✓		✓		✓		✓
Renovator		✓	✓					✓	✓							✓	✓			✓		✓
Reporter	✓										✓					✓	✓		✓			✓
Restorer		✓	✓					✓	✓							✓	✓			✓		✓
Retail Manager				✓	✓						✓								✓		✓	
Retail Assistant					✓														✓	✓		
Roofer			✓					✓									✓			✓		✓
Saddler		✓	✓					✓								✓		✓		✓		✓
Sailor		✓													✓		✓			✓		
Sales Executive				✓													✓		✓			
Sales Manager				✓			✓				✓						✓		✓		✓	
Sales Person				✓													✓		✓			
Sales Trainer				✓	✓						✓					✓	✓		✓			
Science Teacher				✓			✓				✓	✓		✓			✓			✓		
Science Writer	✓			✓							✓		✓			✓	✓			✓		✓
Scientific Instrument Maker		✓	✓				✓	✓			✓			✓			✓		✓		✓	
Scriptwriter	✓										✓					✓	✓					✓
Sculptor		✓					✓									✓	✓		✓			✓
Secretary/PA	✓	✓									✓					✓		✓		✓		
Securities Analyst				✓	✓		✓				✓				✓		✓					✓
Security Officer			✓												✓		✓		✓	✓		✓
Session Musician		✓														✓	✓			✓		
Set Designer		✓					✓									✓	✓		✓			✓
Shipping and Forwarding Officer				✓			✓				✓				✓			✓				
Shop Fitter		✓	✓					✓							✓							
Signwriter		✓						✓								✓		✓		✓		✓
Silversmith		✓						✓								✓		✓		✓		✓
Social Scientist	✓			✓			✓				✓		✓	✓	✓					✓		
Social Worker							✓									✓		✓	✓	✓		
Soldier			✓												✓		✓			✓		
Solicitor	✓							✓			✓	✓		✓		✓		✓		✓		
Sound Engineer		✓		✓											✓			✓				✓
Special Needs Teacher							✓										✓		✓			
Speech Therapist							✓									✓	✓		✓			✓
Sports Coach			✓				✓										✓		✓		✓	
Sports Official Referee			✓														✓		✓			✓
Sports Teacher			✓				✓								✓		✓		✓		✓	
Stagehand		✓						✓								✓	✓			✓		✓
Stage Manager		✓			✓											✓	✓		✓			
Statistician				✓	✓			✓				✓			✓			✓		✓		✓

	W	A	P	E	O	B	S	Ve	F	P	V	N	O	C	F	I	Sp	D	A	P	G	So
Stock Controller					✓		✓					✓			✓		✓		✓			✓
Stockbroker				✓	✓	✓	✓					✓			✓	✓			✓			
Stone Mason		✓						✓							✓	✓				✓		
Studio Assistant		✓													✓	✓				✓		
Stunt Performer			✓					✓	✓						✓	✓			✓			✓
Surgeon				✓				✓			✓	✓			✓		✓		✓			✓
Surveyor		✓		✓			✓	✓							✓		✓		✓			✓
Systems Analyst				✓	✓		✓					✓	✓	✓	✓		✓					
Tailor		✓					✓	✓				✓			✓	✓						✓
Tax Inspector				✓			✓					✓			✓		✓		✓			✓
Taxi Driver			✓				.												✓			✓
Taxidermist		✓						✓							✓	✓						✓
Teacher						✓				✓					✓		✓		✓			✓
Teacher of Art/craft		✓				✓		✓		✓						✓	✓		✓			✓
Teacher of Physically Disabled						✓													✓			
Technical Illustrator		✓		✓			✓	✓				✓			✓		✓		✓			✓
Technical Representative			✓	✓		✓	✓					✓		✓		✓		✓				✓
Technical Writer		✓		✓			✓				✓	✓			✓		✓		✓			✓
Telecommunications Engineer			✓	✓				✓			✓	✓			✓				✓			✓
Telephonist	✓						✓									✓	✓					✓
Television Engineer			✓	✓			✓	✓	✓						✓				✓			✓
Television Production Assistant		✓														✓	✓		✓			
Thatcher			✓					✓							✓		✓		✓			✓
Theatre Administrator		✓		✓			✓		✓	✓					✓		✓				✓	
Tiler			✓				✓								✓		✓		✓			✓
Tool Maker			✓				✓	✓							✓		✓		✓			✓
Toy Maker		✓					✓								✓		✓					
Traffic Warden			✓												✓		✓		✓			✓
Train Driver			✓												✓		✓		✓			✓
Train Engineer			✓	✓				✓	✓						✓		✓					✓
Train Guard			✓															✓	✓			✓
Training Officer	✓			✓		✓				✓		✓			✓		✓		✓			
Translator	✓											✓		✓	✓	✓			✓			✓
Transport Manager			✓			✓									✓		✓		✓			
Travel Agent		✓		✓			✓				✓	✓			✓		✓					
Truck Driver			✓															✓		✓		✓
Turf Accountant					✓		✓					✓			✓		✓		✓			
Umpire			✓			✓											✓	✓				✓
Underwriter				✓			✓					✓	✓	✓	✓		✓		✓			
Union Negotiator						✓											✓	✓				
Upholsterer		✓					✓	✓							✓	✓			✓			✓
Urban Planner		✓		✓			✓	✓			✓				✓		✓		✓			

	W	A	P	E	O	B	S	Ve	F	P	V	N	O	C	F	I	Sp	D	A	P	G	So
Veterinary Nurse			✓												✓			✓		✓		
Veterinary Surgeon			✓	✓				✓	✓		✓	✓			✓			✓				
Vision Mixer		✓		✓					✓			✓				✓		✓		✓		
Vocational Counsellor							✓				✓			✓	✓					✓		
Waiter/Waitress		✓					✓									✓	✓			✓		
Watch Repairer			✓					✓	✓	✓					✓			✓		✓		✓
Welder			✓						✓					✓				✓				
Window Dresser		✓							✓							✓	✓			✓		
Work Study Officer			✓	✓				✓			✓		✓		✓			✓	✓			✓
Writer	✓										✓			✓		✓	✓					✓
Youth Worker					✓															✓	✓	
Zoo Keeper		✓		✓					✓						✓							✓
Zoologist				✓				✓	✓			✓	✓		✓			✓		✓		✓

Explanation of test items

Verification

Tip: With this type of problem, as the strings or chains get longer, it can be helpful to find a reference point in the chain and count the maximum number of items from this until the next reference point. Often, it is easy to perceive from a quick glance at the problem that there is, for example, a double letter, number or symbol that you can count from. Make this the reference point. Then, you will detect where there must be missing elements when you find a sequence with a number less than that required by the repeating sequence.

1. The letters A B are repeated, but in the middle of the chain two B's are together and the A has been missed, so the answer is d).

2. The numbers 2 1 are repeated, but two 2's are together in the middle of the chain, so that a 1 has been missed. Therefore, the answer is f).

3. A single black square is followed by two circles. As there should be two circles in between the two black squares in the middle of the chain, the answer is e).

4. The sequence A B C is repeated, but at one point a C has been left out, so the answer is c).

5. The sequence is a repetition of the two numbers 1 5, but at one point a 1 has been left out, so the answer is f).

6. The sequence square, circle, squiggles is repeated, but on the third repetition the square is missing, so the answer is f).

7. The sequence is C C A B even though C C A has not appeared at the beginning of the chain. Two C's should appear together, but in the middle of the chain this does not happen so that a C is missing and the answer is therefore a).

8. The sequence is 7 6 8 7. Nothing is missing from the middle of the chain, but a 7 is missing from either end, so that the only possible answer from those provided is d).

9. The sequence is two lots of squiggles, a square and a circle. A circle is missing after one of the squares in the middle of the chain, so the answer is e).

10. The sequence is two J's, two T's, followed by a single J and T. In the middle of the chain there is a single J where there should be two, so the answer is d). This is the best answer even though there is a T missing from both ends of the sequence; if you gave the answer 'a)' you would not have made allowance for the missing J.

11. The sequence is 6 1 6 3 3. Within the chain a 6 is missing so the answer is b).

12. The sequence is ♎ ♎ ♒ ♋ ♋. At one point in the chain only a single, not a double ♎ has been printed, so the answer is a).

13. The sequence is R C E D E R. Two of these letters have been left out in the middle of the chain. These are R R, so the answer is f).

14. The sequence is 3 3 6 1 6. A 6 that should follow the double 3 has been omitted from the chain, so the answer is b).

15. The sequence is □ □ ○ □ ♌ ♎. In the chain a circle and a square ○ □ that should follow the two squares □ □ are missing, so the answer is b).

16. The sequence is A B B C C. At a point in the chain A B is missing, so the answer is d).

17. The sequence is 1 1 3 3 8. At a point in the chain a 1 and a 3 are missing, so the answer is a).

18. The sequence is ● ● □ □ ● □.The missing part is given in brackets.

□ ● □ ● ● □ □ ● □ ● ● □ □ ● □ ● ● □ □ ●
□ ● ● □ □ ● □ ● ● □ □ ● (□ ●) ● □

19. The sequence is W R Y W Y R S. The missing part is given in brackets.

W R Y W Y R S W R Y W Y R S W R Y W Y R S W R (Y) W Y

20. The sequence is: 2 2 8 2 3 2 8 2 2 8 2 3 2 (8 2) 2 8 2 3 2 8 2 2 8 2 3 2 8 2 2 8 2 3 2 8

The missing part is given in brackets.

21. The sequence is □ □ ● ● ≋ ●. The missing part is given in brackets.

● ≋ ● □ □ ● (●) ≋ ● □ □ ● ● ≋ ● □ □ ● ●
≋ ● □ □ ● ● ≋ ● □ □

22. The sequence is R T Y U. The missing part is given in brackets.

R T Y U R T Y U R T Y U R T Y U R T (Y U) R T Y

23. The sequence is 6 9 6 3 7 3 . The missing part is given in brackets.

6 9 6 3 7 3 6 9 6 3 7 3 6 (9 6) 3 7 3 6 9 6 3 7 3 6 9 6 3 7 3 6 9

24. The sequence is □ □ ♋ ♋ ♎ ◸. The missing part is given in brackets.

♎ ◸ □ □ ♋ ♋ ♎ ◸ □ □ ♋ ♋ ♎ ◸ □ □ ♋ ♋
♎ ◸ □ □ ♋ ♋ ♎ ◸ □ (□ ♋) ♋ ♎ ◸ □ □

25. The sequence is B T B Y S. The missing part is given in brackets.

B T B Y S B T B Y S B T B Y S B T B Y S B T (B) Y S B T

26. The sequence is 7 7 4 6 7 6 6 4. The missing part is given in brackets.

4 7 7 4 6 7 6 6 4 7 (7 4) 6 7 6 6 4 7 7 4 6 7 6 6 4 7 7 4 6 7 6 6 4 7

27. The sequence is □ ♋ ♋ ♎ □ □ ♋ ♎ ♎. The missing part is given in brackets.

□ ♋ ♋ ♎ □ □ ♋ ♎ ♎ □ ♋ ♋ ♎ □ □ ♋ ♎ ♎
□ ♋ ♋ ♎ □ □ ♋ ♎ ♎ □ ♋ ♋ ♎ □ □ ♋ ♎ ♎
□ ♋ ♋ ♎ □ (□) ♋ ♎ ♎ □ ♋ ♋ ♎

28. The sequence is T T B E S B T E S B. The missing part is given in brackets.

   T B E S B T E S B T T B E S B T E S B T T B E S B T E S B T T
   B E S B T E S B T T B E S B T E S B T T B E S B (T E) S B T T
   B E S B T E S B

29. The sequence is 7 9 1 2 7 4 1. The missing part is given in brackets.

   7 9 1 2 7 4 1 7 9 1 2 7 4 1 7 9 1 2 7 4 1 7 9 1 2 7 4 1 7 9 1 2
   7 4 1 7 9 1 2 7 4 1 7 9 1 2 7 4 (1 7) 9 1 2 7 4 1 7 9 1 2 7 4 1 7
   9 1 2 7 4 1 7 9 1 2 7 4 1 7

30. The sequence is ♎ ♎ □ ♋ ♎ □ ♒ ♋. The missing part is given in brackets.

   □ ♋ ♎ □ ♒ (♋ ♎) ♎ □ ♋ ♎ □ ♒ ♋ ♎ ♎ □
   ♋ ♎ □ ♒ ♋ ♎ ♎ □ ♋ ♎ □ ♒ ♋ ♎ ♎ □ ♋ ♎
   □ ♒ ♋ ♎ ♎ □ ♋ ♎ □ ♒ ♋ ♎ ♎ □ ♋

31. The sequence is S S G I S G I G R B S I R G. The missing part is given in brackets.

   S S G I S G I G R B S I R G S S G I S G I G R B S I R G S S G I
   S G I G R B S I R G S S G I S G I G R B S I R G S S G I S G I
   G R B S I R G S S G I S G I G R B S (I) R G S S G I S G I G R
   B S I R G S S G I S G I G R B S I R G S S G I S G I G R B S I R
   G S S G I S G I G R

32. The sequence is 1 0 7 1 3 8 3 7. The missing part is given in brackets.

1 0 7 1 3 (8 3) 7 1 0 7 1 3 8 3 7 1 0 7 1 3 8 3 7 1 0 7 1 3 8 3 7
1 0 7 1 3 8 3 7 1 0 7 1 3 8 3 7 1 0 7 1 3 8 3 7 1 0 7 1 3 8 3 7
1 0 7 1 3 8 3 7 1 0 7 1 3 8 3 7 1 0 7 1 3 8 3 7 1 0 7 1 3 8 3 7
1 0

33. The sequence is ♏ ♍ ◆ ♏ ♑ ♍ ❖ ❖ ♎ ◆ ♍ ◆. The missing part is given in brackets.

♎ ◆ ♍ ◆ ♏ ♍ ◆ ♏ ♑ ♍ ❖ ❖ ♎ ◆ ♍ ◆ ♏
♍ ◆ ♏ ♑ ♍ ❖ ❖ ♎ ◆ ♍ ◆ ♏ ♍ ◆ ♏ ♑
♍ ❖ ❖ ♎ ◆ ♍ ◆ (♏ ♍) ◆ ♏ ♑ ♍ ❖ ❖
♎ ◆ ♍ ◆ ♏ ♍ ◆ ♏ ♑ ♍ ❖ ❖ ♎ ◆ ♍
◆ ♏

34. The sequence is K K O L P L P P O L K P L O. The missing part is given in brackets.

P L O K K O L P L P (P O) L K P L O K K O L P L P P O L K
P L O K K O L P L P P O L K P L O K K O L P L P P O L K P
L O K K O L P L P P O L K P L O K K O L P L P P O L K P L
O K K O L P L

35. The sequence is 3 2 9 5 9 5 6 3 6 6 5 9 2 6. The missing part is given in brackets.

3 2 9 5 9 5 6 3 6 6 5 9 2 6 3 2 9 5 9 5 6 (3 6 6) 5 9 2 6 3 2 9 5
9 5 6 3 6 6 5 9 2 6 3 2 9 5 9 5 6 3 6 6 5 9 2 6 3 2 9 5 9 5 6 3
6 6 5 9 2 6 3 2 9 5 9 5 6 3 6 6 5 9 2 6 3 2 9 5 9 5 6 3 6 6 5 9
2 6 3 2 9 5 9 5

36. The sequence is ⭘ ⭘ ■ ⭘ ❖ ♍ ⊠ ⊠ ♍ ❖ ❖ ♌ ❖ ♍. The missing part is given in brackets.

❖ ♌ ❖ ♍ ○ ○ ■ ○ ❖ ♍ ⊠ ⊠ ♍ ❖ ❖ ♌ ❖ ♍ ○
○ ■ ○ ❖ ♍ ⊠ ⊠ ♍ ❖ ❖ (♌ ❖ ♍) ○ ○ ■ ○ ❖
♍ ⊠ ⊠ ♍ ❖ ❖ ♌ ❖ ♍ ○ ○ ■ ○ ❖ ♍ ⊠ ⊠ ♍
❖ ❖ ♌ ❖ ♍ ○ ○ ■ ○ ❖ ♍ ⊠ ⊠ ♍ ❖ ❖ ♌ ❖ ♍
○ ○ ■ ○ ❖ ♍ ⊠

Physical Analysis

1. Answer a) would lead to the beam toppling sideways to the left as the distance of the beam from the left end to arrow B is greater than the distance from the right end of the beam to point B. Similar reasoning rejects answer c) when the beam would topple to the right around supporting arrow C. It would of course, also be possible to remove supporting arrows C and B, but this is not provided as an alternative answer. Answer d) must be rejected as it is impossible, given that answers a) and c) are rejected.

2. Glass is safest when its weight is distributed through its length as opposed to its side. Therefore it is safest in a vertical position although, in a temporary position, it would not be wise to place it vertically in case it fell backwards. Answer c) is correct because in this position there is least pressure on the face of the glass. As a further thought, although you are not given the nature of the floor's surface, answer c) gives the least likelihood of the bottom edge of the glass slipping.

3. Wheel C turns clockwise, B anti-clockwise, A clockwise and therefore D anti-clockwise, so the answer is c).

4. The pressure of water on the dam will increase with depth. Answer c) is correct because this dam has the widest construction in relation to depth, or, resistance increases as depth increases.

5. The same facts apply to this design as to the designs in question 4 and by the same reasoning the answer is c).

6. The weight of an object will always exert a force to turn about a fixing point. This is referred to in mechanics as a 'fulcrum'. In this example the fulcrum is the point on the string where it is hooked. In picture frame B the fulcrum is almost at the top of the frame, whereas the fulcrums in A and C are much lower. In picture B the least force is being exerted away from the wall above the fulcrum, thus keeping frame B flattest against the wall.

7. The path of a ray of light may be altered by the medium through which it travels. If a ray of light hits the surface of glass exactly at ninety degrees to its surface its path will continue to be straight. Otherwise, the ray of light will be turned at an angle to the surface of the glass and continue straight through the body of glass until it meets the next surface of glass when it emerges into the air. At the surface of air to glass the light is bent towards the angle that is less than ninety degrees to the surface of the glass and continues through the glass until at the surface of glass to air it again is bent towards the lesser angle than ninety degrees to the air to glass surface. As the ray of light emerges from the glass it has, unless it has hit the glass at the midpoint at a ninety degree angle, been deflected upwards or downwards through the body of the glass. The purpose of a concave lens is to spread rays apart and any image viewed through such a lens will appear to be smaller than the real object.

8. The driving wheel turns anti-clockwise. All the wheels must therefore turn the same way. For example, the driving wheel pulls the band around the bottom left hand wheel thus turning it anti-clockwise and, in turn, this wheel turns the band around wheel W thus turning it anti-clockwise.

9. Hot air will ascend from the land as this is heated more rapidly than the sea, thus drawing in replacement air from the sea creating an onshore wind.

10. The forces of the wind and tide are opposite, but the force of the wind, if the sailing boat heads straight for Brightport, will not be sufficient to prevent the force of the tide taking the boat to the west. The force of the tide must be counteracted by sailing to the east, but heading D, although somewhat in the right direction, is likely to be too extreme and therefore C is the best answer.

11. Being on the outermost place of the curve C will have travelled furthest in the same time and has therefore travelled fastest.

12. As the intervals between each car entering the bend are not given it is not possible to say how fast car A or car B had to go in order to catch car C, so d) is the correct answer.

13. The time shown by the clock is regulated by the rate of the pendulum, which beats more slowly as it is lengthened. As the clock is running late, the pendulum must be caused to beat more rapidly and therefore the weight must be adjusted upwards, answer b).

14. If she is at A, the sailor will have placed her weight to counteract the heeling force of the wind as she hauls the sails. Position B does not have this advantage and C even less so. In fact, the more the sailor's weight moves from port to starboard (right) the greater is the chance of the dinghy capsizing due to the effect of both her weight and the wind increasing the heeling motion, and the additional danger of drifting onto a lee shore.

15. The force of gravity on the bar will roll the tube up the slope.

16. The bands passing around each wheel draw all other wheels in the same manner as F.

17. The cylinders will rest in such a way that most weight is at the bottom of each one. Although C has weight on either side of the cylinder when looking at the face, rather like saddle-bags, most weight is still in the lower half.

18. The wheel that turns the most times will be the one with the smallest circumference. D will only have turned about a quarter of a turn to allow the band to turn G fully around.

19. Water is pulled by gravity towards the moon, the action of which creates tides.

20. Gravitational pull of the sun will pull the rock towards it thus altering its course.

21. A allows the most even heating within the boiler. Hot water rises, which is why it is drawn off from the top of the heater. Introduction of cold water at A (next best place) has the disadvantage of drawing off water from D before it is heated to the same temperature throughout the heater, because the water to the left of the heater may not receive an equal pressure from the flow of the boiler. The same disadvantage lies with B and E whereas at C it is possible that cold water introduced at this point will be drawn off before it is heated by the hot water beneath it.

22. As the actual surface on which its wheels are placed are flat and not tilted, as though it was going down a hill, it is likely to remain in the same position.

23. Rays of light from the ball to the man's eyes are deflected at the pool's surface. From the man's point of view the light will have bent downwards through the water.

24. Due to the length of its outside edge, the 'circumference', C will travel furthest in the time.given. C will win as it needs fewer revolutions to complete the race.

25. D moves anti-clockwise. As the band is crossed before it turns C, C moves clockwise. B moves clockwise in the same manner as C. The band is again crossed before it gets from B to A and therefore B's clockwise rotation is transferred to an anti-clockwise rotation.

26 The effect of this type of prism is to spread white light through its different wavelengths so that emerging light from the prism is displayed throughout the range of primary colours (red, orange, yellow, green, blue, indigo, violet) and thus from different points on the surface of the prism, so that h) is the best answer.

27. As B has the smaller surface area, it retains heat better than A, and therefore cools more slowly.

28. Looking at the diagram, M, when turning as shown, has the effect of its slanted surface moving from right to left across the page, or anti-clockwise if viewed from underneath or the flat face of the gear. This action turns the gear it is touching so that the slanted surface moves down the page, or clockwise if viewed from the side of the gear. In turn, this action rotates gear H so that its slanted surface moves from left to right across the page, or anti-clockwise, direction A, when viewed from the top or the flat surface of the gear.

Verbal penetration

Tip: Words can have many meanings. You therefore have to connect the particular meaning of the words in the question in relation to the associative meaning of the words in the answers. This is how depth of vocabulary provides one basis for abstract thinking. Examples of words that are opposite or the same (antonyms or synonyms) can be found in a thesaurus. Otherwise a dictionary should be consulted for the meanings of words.

1.   A pebble is a single item and a beach is a place where a collection may be found. The same principle holds for a tree in relation to a forest.

2.   Slow is the opposite of prompt, punctual, immediate, timely.

3.   As bacon is the meat of pig, so mutton is the meat of sheep.

4.   A chip is a part of something else. It can be part of a potato or piece of wood, but these alternatives do not describe chip or fragment.

5.   Dawn and noon are points in time, as are dusk and midnight. Other alternatives are vague.

6.   Feathers would not be related to fish, whilst tail and fins are specific parts rather than the outside surface as in the case of hair on a dog.

7.   One of the meanings of tail is to track, keep up with, stalk or follow.

8.   Sock and glove are both covers, but the specific part of the body is hand. It is not fingers because foot is part of the question not toes. Pocket is incorrect because it can be a

receptacle for many things and is not designed to go on the part of the body as in the case of sock or glove.

9. Blunt means without artifice, so alternatives for blunt are direct, outspoken and forthright.

10. Steadfast can mean the same as true, but is not the opposite of disagreeable. Cheer and qualify are either nouns or verbs rather than an adjective as are pleasant and disagreeable.

11. All, bar an autocrat, have a belief in participatory government.

12. Hoof and paw are both the forefoot of the animals.

13. Exhaust is to wear out, whereas liven is to invigorate.

14. Not to be mislead by aspects of the story of 'The Prodigal Son', the word prodigal means wasteful or excessive.

15. All begin with 'm'. All have 'a' as the second letter. The 'n' in d) comes before the 'u' in all the others, so d) must come first. The 'n' in a) comes before the 'v' and 's' in b) and c) so a) must come second. The 's' in mausoleum comes before the 'v' in mauve, so c) comes third in alphabetical order.

16. To scale is to climb and only descent means the act of going downwards, which is the opposite. Although descent is a noun and scale is a verb, so is ascent a noun and descend a verb.

17. Only d) does not mean plentiful.

18. The question is with what form water can take in particular circumstances or at certain temperatures so that water, cloud or rain do not describe the form of steam with sufficient accuracy.

19. Ill-temper are all described by a), b) and c).

20. Humour, as a verb, means to indulge, be kind to or coax.

21. Sparse is an adjective meaning that the items described appear infrequently, wheareas abundant is an adjective meaning plentiful.

22. The consequence of to ignite and to trigger are to catch fire and to set something off. In the first instance the consequence is burning and in the second the consequence is a change or reaction.

23. To boost is to improve or increase whilst degrade is decrease or worsen. To applaud is to praise whilst to humiliate is to deride or shame.

24. Oblivious means regardless or unaware, which is the opposite of observant, heedful or watchful.

25. All but c) describe an attack, insult or ill-treatment.

26. The question concerns the item that is the focus of study of that branch of science.

27. Only d) does not contain the concept of togetherness.

28. A stanza is part of a poem as a movement is part of a symphony. Movement, in some form, exists in all the other answers but not in the relationship in which it is a precisely defined section or part of a composition.

29. A plosive is an expiration or breathing out.

30. To chivvy is to urge or hurrying something up, which is the same as to chase. To seek is to look for, to pursue or to inquire.

31. The common concept is that of a collection, of which birds belong to a flock and subjects, or individuals, to a populace.

32. The stock describes what is always available and is therefore not unusual.

33. A donor and philanthropist share the act of giving whereas a recipient and legatee are both beneficiaries.

34. Only a) describes a state that is weakened or is wanting in energy.

35. The common concept is in what is transitory – with what does not last very long.

36. One word in each pair may be grammatically and meaning-fully replaced by the other.

37. To sap is to undermine, or take away from, whereas brace is to buttress or support.

38. Quenched means extinguished or exhausted, whereas all the other words describe liveliness.

39. All but d) describe poor, unremarkable quality.

40. The concepts are with rapidity of action and incautiousness as opposed to measured, thoughtful evaluation.

41. The concepts are with holding back or hiding as opposed to going forward or clarifying.

42. All but c) describe belongingness or things of the same type.

Numerical deduction

Tip: sometimes more than one possible answer could, in theory, be calculated from a sequence of numbers, but the correct one must be in the alternatives provided. Therefore, where you find the sequence itself difficult, it can help to try out each of the possible answers to see if it works.

1. 0 (+5) 5 (+5) 10 (+5) 15 (+5) 20 (+5) ?

2. .25 (×2) .5 (×2) 1 (×2) 2 (×2) 4 (×2) ?

3. 98 (÷2+1) 50 (÷2+1) 26 (÷2+1) 14 (÷2+1) 8 (÷2+1) ?

4. 1 (+1) 2 (1+2) 3 (2+3) 5 (3+5) 8 (5+8) ?

5. 4 (+4) 8 (+4) 12 (+4) 16 (+4) 20 (+4) ?

6. 160 (−40) 120 (−40÷2=−20) 100 (−20÷2=−10) 90 (−10÷2=−5) 85 (−5÷2=−2.5) ?

7. .55 (+0.1) .65 (+0.1) .75 (+0.1) .85 (+0.1) .95 (+0.1) ?

8. 1 (1×2+1=3) 3 (3×2+2=8) 8 (8×2+3=19) 19 (19×2+4=42) 42 (42×2+5=) ?

9. 2 (+5) 7 (+5) 12 (+5) 17 (+5) 22 (+5) ?

10. 1 (+6) 7 (+6) 13 (+6) 19 (+6) 25 (+6) ?

11. 3 (3×3−1=8) 8 (8×3−2=22) 22 (22×3−3=63) 63 (63×3−4=185) 185 (185×3−5=) ?

12. 7 (0) 7 (2) 9 (2+2) 13 (2+2+2) 19 (2+2+2+2) ?

13. 1 (0) 1 (+1) 2 (+2) 4 (+3) 7 (+4) ?

14. 0 (−1) −1 (+1) 0 (+3) 3 (+5) 8 (+7) ?

15. 0 3 (0+3) 3 (3+3) 6 (3+6) 9 (6+9) ?

16. 6 (+3) 9 (−6) 3 (+5) 8 (−5) 3 (+7) ?

17. 7 (+5) 12 (−3) 9 (+10) 19 (−6) 13 (+15 or 20) ?

    Only d) is possible from the answers provided.

18. 75 (−25) 50 (+40) 90 (−25) 65 (+40) 105 (−25) ?

19. 3 (+6) 9 (−5) 4 (+12) 16 (−5) 11 (+12, 18 or 24) ?

    Only d) is possible from the answers provided.

20. 17 11 (17+11) 28 (11+28) 39 (28+39) 67 (39+67) ?

21. 5 (−2) 3 (1) 4 (5) 9 (14) 23 (37) ?

Observation

1. The triangle is white then black and is turned upside down. The opposing quadrilateral would be expected to be white and turned the other way up, thus a).

2. A circle moves from the right centre face of a square to the top right face of the square and then to the right of the top face of the square apparently alternating as it moves from being black to white with successive movements. The next position should be at the centre of the top face of the square when it should also be white, thus c).

3. Drawing a line from the centre of each of the figures within the circles would require a clockwise direction in all but c).

4. To make a) the first triangle would have to be turned upside down, with c) it would need to be turned sideways and with d) it would also need to be turned upside down. Answer a) puts the triangles together in the same orientation.

5. The arrow moves regularly from 3 o'clock, 6, 9 and 12 o'clock. It should move next to 3 o'clock, answer a).

6. The circles and shading are reversed so that where there is black there is now white, thus c).

7. The answer cannot be a) because there is no reason to suggest that the square should change to white and hide the circle when they are put together. Similarly, it could only be c) if there were evidence to support the complete covering of the circle. Again, d) would require the reduction in the size of the square and there is no suggestion this should be so. Answer b) puts both figures together in a logical and least tortuous manner.

8. As the line moves successively from top right, top left, bottom left and bottom right anti-clockwise around the square, it would be expected next again at the top right hand corner of the square, answer d). There is no reason it should be a) or b) as the line is never against the side of the square as it moves around, and in c) it would have had to have moved twice, not once as is the rule.

9. All but c) are irregular, have different shapes, sides or are tilted.

10. The illustrative figure has been flipped over, that is, the bottom has gone to the top and the right has gone to the left. This movement takes place with answer b) in relation to the figure.

11. The white circle within the black border of the smaller figure fits over the white inner circle of the larger figure but the white frame still appears around the black circle when they are added together, as in answer a).

12. Only c) has a circle and a square on the same side of a line. No other criteria are so simple and convincing.

13. The right triangle progresses over the left triangle. As they are the same size, on the third succession the points of both triangles must be touching the right or left sides of the opposing triangles. On the next move the points must move equally across these sides, as in d).

14. In the example the large square has turned so that its base is horizontal, whilst the white square has been replaced by a black circle in the centre of the square. It would be expected that the large square in the next figure would turn the same way so that it finishes by being on a corner, whilst the white circle would become black. This eliminates c) and d). As a square may turn into a circle of a different shade in an inside figure and it may be expected that circles similarly turn into squares, would eliminate a). The outside figure obviously does not change its shape only its alignment. We therefore expect to see a small black square with a horizontal base within a white square that is on a corner, thus b).

15. Only in a) are the same number of sides of the inner figure the same as the outer one, whilst all the others are less.

16. The figures are rotating anti-clockwise. At the same time the line with the black circle takes turns with the arrow and the white circle. The next figure would be a vertical line with a black circle at the bottom, thus b).

17. In the example, the four sides of the smaller figure on the left becomes five in the figure on the right, whilst the three sides of the figure on the left becomes four sides in the right hand figure. Therefore, we expect that a large five sided figure that contains a six sided figure would become a six sided large figure containing a smaller figure of seven sides, thus d).

18. The first three figures suggest that a line with a circle is followed by a plain line. The next figure is most likely to be a straight line, which eliminates a) and b) even though a) would seem to be in the orientation we would expect. The answer c) is better than d) for two reasons: because anti-clockwise rotation is suggested by the sequence and because the two lines with circles are in a different relationship.

19. Only c) shows all the lines of the two original figures in the correct orientation.

20. b), c) and d) are identical although they have been turned around, whereas a) has been turned over.

21. The line with the black square turns anti-clockwise around its middle point and around the middle point of the line with the white circle. In its first position it lies along the line with the white circle so that the square covers the circle. Then it moves vertically, then horizontally and then again vertically with the black square now at the bottom. The next movement will see a horizontal alignment with the black square again covering the white circle, thus d). It cannot be a) because the black square has moved but the line has remained in its previous position.

22. The white circles must be at the top and to the right of their lines.

23. All but d) have one incomplete shape.

24. The lateral lines in both figures extend as far down the page as the vertical lines they touch. Only c) shows these lines correctly and also includes all other parts of both figures.

25. In the example, the 'flag' is at the top left of the line and then at the bottom right whilst the line itself is turned by ninety degrees. We would expect the following figure to be turned by ninety degrees and the 'flag' to move from bottom left to top right, thus b).

26. In the second drawing a black ball has been added to the left of the white ball and in the third drawing a white ball has been added to the left of the black ball. What follows next most logically is that a black ball should be added to the left of the white ball, thus a).

27. a) and b) have a horizontal line at the top of the joined figures, which cannot be correct as there is no such line in the original drawings. d) shows part of the left hand triangle of the original right hand drawing hidden by the triangle of the original left hand drawing, whilst at the same time the black circle overlaps both triangles, which is a contradiction. Only c) shows all parts of both the original drawing in their correct relationship.

28. The black circle is moving anti-clockwise around the lines two sticks at a time, whilst the white circle moves clockwise one stick at a time. In the next drawing we would expect the black circle to have moved on two sticks to the left of the vertical and the white circle to have moved on once to the right of the vertical, thus d).

29. The horizontal line moves from the horizontal, vertically, horizontally, and therefore we would expect it to be vertical next time. At the same time, the white circle is top left, bottom left and still bottom left, so that we cannot be sure whether it will remain in the same position or move back to the top left as in a) or bottom right as in c). This reasoning therefore will not work. Alternatively, imagining the bottom half of the first drawing as a half 'plate', it moves a quarter of a turn anti-clockwise to its position in the second drawing where it hides the top right circle but reveals the bottom left circle. In the third drawing it has again moved a quarter of a turn anti-clockwise so that it continues to hide the top circle and still leaves the bottom left hand circle exposed. Next we would expect the covering 'plate' to have moved around a quarter turn so that it is on the left hand side of the circle, which would reveal the top right hand circle and cover the bottom left hand circle, thus a).

30. c) is the only one not to have a circle as well as a right angled figure.

31. As in 29 above, it is helpful to imagine the circles as containing three surfaces: as the little circles are sometimes covered, these must be on the lowest surface; they are covered by half circular 'plates'. One of the plates is also covered by another 'plate' so that at the bottom there are little circles, then a 'plate' in the middle level and then a top 'plate'. It can be seen from the drawings that the top 'plate' moves from side to side hiding everything underneath it, whilst the middle plate must move around a quarter of a turn each time because it has the same alignment with the top 'plate' in the first and third drawings. In the first drawing both 'plates' are on the left revealing top and bottom circles to the right. In the second drawing the top 'plate' has moved to the other side thus covering the two circles on the right whilst the 'plate' under-

neath it has moved clockwise a quarter turn revealing a small circle at bottom left but covering the presumed small circle at top left. In the third drawing the top 'plate' has moved back to the left side whilst the plate underneath has moved a quarter turn so that both plates cover all circles. In the fourth drawing the top plate has moved to the right hand side whilst the 'plate' underneath has moved clockwise a quarter turn so that the plates only reveal the top left circle. Next, we would expect to see the top plate on the left hand side, the plate underneath also on the left hand side having moved on clockwise a quarter turn and thus directly underneath the top 'plate' so that the circles at top right and bottom left are revealed, thus a).

32. The figure is 'flipped over' on its axis and then rotated anti-clockwise 90 degrees.

33. The half circular 'plate' with the black circle moves clockwise a quarter turn each time so that we would expect it to be top right at the next instance, thus eliminating b) and d). The 'plate' on which there is a white circle appears to move half a turn in an anti-clockwise direction each time so that in the next instance we would expect it to be at bottom left of the circle, thus eliminating b) and c), whilst d) does not seem to present the white circle in the correct position. a) is the only remaining possibility, however, looking further at what appears to be a middle 'plate', this seems to be plain, that is, without circles, and also seems to move from one side to the other each time. It may be envisioned exactly under the 'plate' with the black circle in the first drawing, its top part

appearing in the second drawing, then appearing fully in the third drawing where the black circle 'plate' completely covers the one with the white circle black, and then its lower half appearing in the fourth drawing. In the next instance the plain 'plate' would have moved to the right hand side, but is, in fact, covered by the 'plate' with the black circle. Therefore, a) remains the only possible answer.

34. Only in d) is one of the internal lines drawn from the other internal line.

35. The black circle moves back and forth so that in the next instance it will be top right, which appears in all the alternatives. The white circle moves anti-clockwise, but when it moves to the same position as the black circle it is hidden by the black circle, so that in the next instance it should be top right, which eliminates c) and d). The triangle between the two lines alternates so that on the next occasion it will be on the right, which happens for all alternatives. The small white circle, seen between the two lines in the first drawing, moves a quarter of a turn anti-clockwise. In the second drawing it is hidden by the triangle. In the continuing – fifth instance- it should have come around to the top again between the two lines so it cannot be a), thus b) where it is positioned correctly and because b) is not eliminated by the other criteria.

Critical dissection

1.   EAST   WEST

      Mr Smith   Mr Brown   Mr Burton

2. and 3.

	Susan	Stella	Sukie	Sally
Pizza	Y	Y		
Pasta			Y	Y
Lasagne	Y			Y

4. LEAST MOST

Chris Fred (Peter Joan Jack)

5. and 6.

	Toby	Rob	Frank	Sam	Jo	Tony
Packed lunch	Y	Y	Y			
Canteen meal				Y	Y	Y
Bus			Y	Y	Y	
Married		Y			Y	Y

7. and 8.

	SLOWEST		FASTEST	
Before training:	Janet	Marcus		Eric Angela
After training:	Marcus		Eric	Janet Angela

9. and 10.

	Fred	Joe	John	Garth
Full-time	Y		Y	
Part-time		Y		Y
Train		Y	Y	
Walk	Y			Y
Own cars	Y	Y		

11. and 12.

Information given:	Therefore:
The Horse's Mouth is above *The Winter's Tale*	*The Wind in the Willows* (top shelf)
The Last Days of the Third Reich is above *A Book of Practical Cats*	*The Horse's Mouth, Justine*
The Wind in the Willows (top shelf)	*The Winter's Tale, The Last Days of the Third Reich*
The Horse's Mouth is on the same shelf *as Justine*	*A Book of Practical Cats*
A Winter's Tale is above *A Book of Practical Cats*	

13., 14. and 15.

	Casey	Stuart	Ritchie	Billie	Colin
Own Desk	Y	Y	Y	Y	Y
Computer	Y				Y
Calculators		Y	Y	Y	
Manual	Y		Y		
Instructions	Y	Y	Y	Y	Y
Wood desk	Y			Y	
Metal desk		Y	Y		Y

16., 17., 18. and 19.

	Sharon	Kelly	Robina	Sam
Corn	Y	Y		Y
Beans		Y		Y
Fish	Y		Y	
Tomatoes	Y		Y	
Potatoes	Y	Y		

20., 21. and 22.

	Mr Bagshaw	Miss Jenkins	Mrs Chance	Mr Fleming	Mr Marx
Blue car	Y				Y
Red car		Y	Y	Y	
White stripe	Y		Y		
Blue stripe		Y			
Orange stripe				Y	Y
White upholstery	Y		Y		Y
Blue upholstery		Y		Y	

23., 24. and 25.

	WINNERS			
LOSERS	Quaid	Jones	Barlow	Moorcock
Quaid			WIN	
Jones	WIN		WIN	
Barlow				
Moorcock	WIN	WIN	WIN	

26., 27., 28. and 29.

	Sally	Cheryl	Laura	Tom	Sandy
Fudge	Y*		Y*	Y*	Y*
Chocolate	Y		Y		Y
Fruit gum		Y			
Toffee			Y	Y	

* Four of them take a piece of fudge and because Cheryl only takes one sweet, a fruit gum, this must be all the others.

30., 31., 32. and 33.

	Penknife			Key			Book		
	Light	Fairly heavy	Very heavy	Light	Fairly heavy	Very heavy	Light	Fairly heavy	Very heavy
John	Y(iii)				Y(ii)				Y(iv)
Rick		Y(ii)				Y(iv)	Y(iii)		
Ted			Y	Y(i)				Y(i)	

(i) Ted's penknife is a very heavy one. His key is not a fairly heavy one and cannot be very heavy because he already has a heavy object, his penknife, so it must be light, and, therefore, it must be the book that is fairly heavy.

(ii) Ted's book, Rick's penknife and John's key are all described the same way so, as it has been established that Ted's book is fairly heavy, the others must be too.

(iii) Rick's book and John's penknife are the same weight. John's penknife must be the light one because the fairly heavy one belongs to Rick and the very heavy one to Ted.

(iv) These are the only remaining possibilities that can complete the matrix, giving each boy the same objects each with three different weights.